INSIGHT ⊙ GUIDES

GREAT BREAKS

BRIGHTON, SUSSEX & THE SOUTH DOWNS

D1341600

 Walking Eye App

Your Insight Guide purchase includes a free download of the destination's corresponding eBook. It is available now from the free Walking Eye container app in the App Store and Google Play. Simply download the Walking Eye container app to access the eBook dedicated to your purchased book. The app also features free information on local events taking place and activities you can enjoy during your stay, with the option to book them. In addition, premium content for a wide range of other destinations is available to purchase in-app.

EBOOKS

EVENTS

ACTIVITIES

SETTINGS

ABOUT

HOW TO DOWNLOAD THE WALKING EYE APP

Available on purchase of this guide only.
1. Visit our website: www.insightguides.com/walkingeye
2. Download the Walking Eye container app to your smartphone (this will give you access to your free eBook and the ability to purchase other products)
3. Select the scanning module in the Walking Eye container app
4. Scan the QR Code on this page – you will be asked to enter a verification word from the book as proof of purchase
5. Download your free eBook* for travel information on the go

* Other destination apps and eBooks are available for purchase separately or are free with the purchase of the Insight Guide book

Contents

Walks and Tours

Brighton, Sussex and the South Downs's Top 10

From the bracing hills of the Downs to historic sights and fashionable seaside resorts, this scenic and varied part of England has much to offer

▲ **Royal Pavilion.** This outrageously extravagant seaside palace was built for the Prince Regent in the 1810s. See page 23.

▲ **Brighton Festival.** One of Britain's biggest and most varied arts festivals, with drama, comedy and music staged in venues throughout the town. See page 30.

▲ **South Downs Way.** Britain's first designated long-distance bridleway and a popular path for walkers of all abilities. See page 48.

▶ **Lewes.** The scene of battles since Saxon times and today best known for its explosive Guy Fawkes celebrations. See page 54.

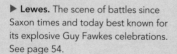

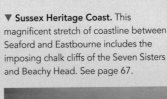

▼ **Sussex Heritage Coast.** This magnificent stretch of coastline between Seaford and Eastbourne includes the imposing chalk cliffs of the Seven Sisters and Beachy Head. See page 67.

▲ **Bloomsbury in Sussex.** The Bloomsbury Set started in London but ended up in the country. The former home of Virginia and Leonard Woolf, Monk's House in Rodmell, is now a National Trust property. See page 61.

▼ **Eastbourne seafront.** A fashionable Victorian seaside resort and still a popular tourist destination, this genteel town boasts some fine Victorian buildings along its seafront. See page 71.

▲ **Chichester Cathedral.** Founded in 1076, this Gothic-Romanesque cathedral is known for its graceful interior and vibrant stained glass. See page 84.

▼ **Arundel Wetland Centre.** A beautiful spot to see Sussex wildlife with reed beds, boat safaris and great activities for kids. See page 106.

▲ **Petworth House.** One of England's finest stately homes, and home to paintings by Van Dyck, Gainsborough, Blake and Turner. See page 102.

Ditchling Beacon.

Overview

Where the South Downs Meet the Sea

With fine architecture and bags of character, Brighton is a city that's easy to love. Facing the sea and backed by beautiful Sussex countryside, its setting is hard to beat

Barely 60 miles (97km) from London and under 80 miles (129km) from Normandy, the South Saxon kingdom of Sussex was a region worth

invading. Dotted with the remains of Iron Age forts and Roman walls, it took the brunt of the Norman Conquest in 1066 and has been staunchly defended ever since. The Normans built castles at Chichester, Arundel, Bramber, Lewes, Pevensey and Hastings, the Plantagenets walled in the Cinque Ports of Winchelsea and Rye, and Georgian Martello towers sprang up along the coast during the Napoleonic Wars. Further defences appeared during the world wars and while the barbed wire and bomb sites have long since been cleared, pillboxes, memorials and veterans' settlements remain.

But it's the long intervening years of peace that have left the most en-

during legacy on these hills, valleys and shores. Farmers and fishermen have woven the tapestry of fields, hedgerows, woods and villages visible in East and West Sussex today, with well-connected landowners developing its grand country estates and flourishing towns and cities.

Of these, the largest and most influential is Brighton, a city which made its fortune by offering 18th-, 19th- and 20th-century visitors a breezy, healthy and indulgent respite from London. Today, it embraces a multitude of influences. Part tourist resort, part hub for education, new media and the arts, its broad-minded, up-for-it attitude tends to make a big impression right from the start.

LANDSCAPES

Much of Sussex is protected by the South Downs National Park and by two Areas of Outstanding Natural Beauty, Chichester Harbour and the High Weald. Even beyond these special landscapes, there are fields and

woods to refresh the soul. Newcomers to Sussex are sometimes surprised to find so much open countryside so close to London, let alone to Brighton, which wears the South Downs round its shoulders like a cape.

With thin soil exposed to the salty southwesterlies, the grassy-topped Downs provide grazing for sheep and rabbits and a habitat for rare butterflies and wildflowers. These curvaceous hills are mostly chalk, shaped during the last Ice Age, but here and there you may spot a sarsen stone or greywether, foreign-looking sandstone rocks dating back to the Eocene.

In the valleys, where the earth is richer, skylarks sing over poppy fields, cows and pheasants meander through lush pastures and there are sun-dappled beech woods where bluebells and fungi bloom. The tide-washed coast, meanwhile, is constantly changing. Castles and docks which once looked out to sea have slowly been marooned inland, while else-

The pretty village of Amberley in West Sussex.

where, waves batter the cliffs and fallen chalk paints the water white.

TOWNS AND VILLAGES

Youthful, brash and energetic, Brighton grabs most of the attention in Sussex, but there's much to enjoy and admire in the historic towns of Chichester, Arundel and Lewes. All three have impressive ecclesiastical architecture, appealing Georgian and Regency streets and a distinctive charm that's all their own. Even Eastbourne and Hastings, once considered dull and down-at-heel by some, have had a change in fortunes; both now have sparkling contemporary art galleries and invigorating programmes of events.

The coastal towns of Sussex are diverse, not only in atmosphere, but also in architecture. The Regency terraces of Brighton and Hove are undoubtedly a highlight, but there are also daring splashes of Art Deco, best appreciated at Bexhill's De La Warr Pavilion or, near Brighton, at Shoreham Airport or Saltdean Lido, which is slowly being restored.

Inland, the classic village pattern of pretty cottages, a pub and a church arranged around an ancient scrap of green repeats itself time and time again in both East and West Sussex, with Alfriston, Amberley and East Dean among the most picturesque. While many timber-framed houses were given smart Georgian facades in the 1700s and early 1800s, some of the loveliest old buildings are still walled with lime or flint, sometimes knapped (chipped into a flat-fronted shape) at considerable expense.

Traces of exquisite Roman-era buildings still survive, along with churches with enchanting frescoes and square, squat towers, built by the Saxons. The Normans rebuilt may of these, however, often adding decorated, rounded arches in Caen stone brought over

Guide to Coloured Boxes

Eating	This guide is dotted with coloured boxes providing additional practical and cultural information to make the most of your visit. Here is a guide to the coding system.
Fact	
Green	
Kids	
Shopping	
View	

from France; there are fine examples in Steyning and Amberley.

PEOPLE AND CULTURE

Present-day East and West Sussex can trace their cultural roots back well over 1,000 years. Long isolated from the rest of England by sea, forests and marshes, this is a predominantly rural region that's proud of its independent spirit and aversion to authority. Even today, the populations of Brighton and Lewes are more radical and unconventional than elsewhere in the southeast.

As elsewhere in Britain, most local folk traditions are seasonal celebrations linked to the farming year, but there's one notable exception. The counties are famous for their anarchic autumn bonfire and firework nights, tenuously linked to Guy Fawkes' Gunpowder Plot of 1605, but more firmly connected to the martyrdom of Protestants in Sussex during the previous century. Each gathering is led by a local bonfire society which holds fund-raising events all year round until finally, on a night of raucous madness, the lot goes up in smoke. The celebrations tend to be spaced out over a month or so from early October, with the biggest of all taking place on 5

The Great Outdoors

With huge areas of protected downland, wetlands and woodlands, Sussex is a fantastic destination for nature lovers and outdoor enthusiasts. Chichester Harbour and the seaside towns offer access to the Solent and the English Channel, while the South Downs Way, the only National Trail to run right across a national park, leads through gorgeous countryside, crisscrossed by ancient drovers' paths.

November in Lewes, where 17 Protestants died and the tradition began.

A relatively recent addition to the folk calendar is Sussex Day, 16 June. Marking the occasion in 1276 when St Richard of Chichester, patron saint of Sussex, was enshrined at Chichester Cathedral, it's gradually becoming a day of flag-raising, feasting and village fairs. Historic re-enactments are also something of a local speciality, with a huge medieval festival at Herstmonceux Castle in August and a suitably high-spirited 1066 celebration at Battle in October, featuring over 1,000 costumed soldiers.

Brighton Beach in summertime.

Food and Drink

Traditional Sussex food, though hearty and delicious, is no longer easy to find – so if you're lucky enough to come across straightforward coast-and-country fare such as grilled mackerel, Southdown lamb, beef stew and dumplings, suet pudding or downland rabbit pie on a pub or restaurant menu, it's well worth giving it a try.

Most of the busiest restaurants in Sussex have their focus firmly on contemporary British and fusion dining. When old-fashioned, carb-heavy, butter-laden favourites like Sussex Pond Pudding or Banoffi Pie (the invention of a South Downs restaurant) are on offer, they'll probably be served with an ironic or exotic twist – in a tiny portion, perhaps, with a dollop of crème fraîche, a scribble of coulis and a sprinkle of salted caramel.

Local ingredients, however, have never been more popular. Meat, fish, apples, soft fruit and vegetables from East and West Sussex are all excellent, and the number of Sussex eateries offering good food that's sustainably grown, reared, foraged or harvested is increasing all the time.

FISH AND CHIPS

Fish and chips always taste best eaten straight out of the paper, preferably on a pier or a beach. But for the freshest fish, the tastiest batter and the crunchiest, fluffiest chips, you have to know where to go. In Brighton, The Palm Court, Bardsley's and Bankers

Farm Shops

Brighton Farm Shop, Warren Road, Brighton (www.brightonfarmshop. co.uk). Busy shop near the racecourse on the edge of the city, with daily deliveries from local farmers.

Charlie's Farm Shop, Bury, near Arundel (www.charliesfarmshop. co.uk). Friendly, modern shop on a dairy farm that's been in the same family for around a century.

Cowdray Farm Shop Easebourne, near Midhurst (www.cowdray.co.uk). Excellent shop and café offering award-winnning venison, eggs and produce from the Cowdray Estate and nearby farms.

Crossbush Farm Shop, Crossbush, near Arundel (www.crossbushfarm shop.co.uk). Meat from traditional breeds, seasonal game and a tempting deli.

Eggs to Apples, Hurst Green, High Weald (www.eggstoapples.co.uk). Bright and welcoming, this shop sells a great range of produce including locally grown plants and fresh fish, delivered daily.

Middle Farm, Firle, near Lewes (www.middlefarm.com). One of Britain's original farm shops with a famously fantastic cider and perry barn, a café and an area where kids can meet farm animals.

Runcton Farm Shop, Runcton, near Chichester (www.runctonfarmshop. co.uk). Large shop selling local cheese, meat and produce, with pick-your-own fruit in season.

Rushfields Farm Shop, Poynings, near Brighton (www.rushfields. com). Highly acclaimed for its pies, sausages, artisan bread and cheese.

A hearty portion of fish and chips.

lead the pack. Elsewhere, Osborne's in Seaford, Trident in Eastbourne and the Life Boat in Hastings stand head and shoulders above the rest.

COUNTRY PUBS AND TEA SHOPS

For those moments when you're gasping for a pint or longing for tea with scones, jam and cream, Sussex has gorgeous country boltholes that deliver. Creaky floors, low beams, open fires and sunny gardens are the norm. The cluster of pubs and tea shops in and around Alfriston are particularly special, making this picturesque village an excellent place to begin or end a walk.

FOOD MARKETS AND FESTIVALS

Cows, sheep and goats all thrive on the pastures of the Weald, and specialist stalls at the region's many farmers' markets stock scrumptious artisan cheese such as Sussex Slipcote sheep's cheese and High Weald Dairy Cheddar. Chichester's twice-monthly farmers' market is one of the best – it sells heaps of seasonal fruit, vegetables, chutneys, honey and other treats in a supremely atmospheric setting, beside the Market Cross. Brighton holds a big food festival in August and September, with smaller editions in April, May and December.

VINEYARDS AND BREWERIES

Craft beer and real ale connoisseurs have plenty of homegrown brews to choose from in Sussex. A few breweries, including Langham near Petworth, offer guided tours. Lewes' famous Harveys Brewery runs tours, too, but the waiting list is typically two years long.

Wine drinkers have much to enjoy here. One of the happier consequences of climate change is that Sussex is well on the way to becoming a vine-growing region to rival Champagne. The Breaky Bottom, Stopham and Ridgeview wine estates all have an excellent reputation and newcomer Rathfinny near Alfriston is definitely one to watch. There's always a good selection of local vintages for sale at the English Wine Centre in Berwick.

Eating Out Price Guide

Typical main course for one person.
£££ = over £15
££ = £10–15
£ = under £10

Sunbathing on Brighton Beach.

The entrance to
Brighton Pier.

Tour 1

Central Brighton

Tap into the energy of the city by the sea on this walk around central Brighton, relaxing on the seafront, wandering through The Lanes and visiting the Royal Pavilion

In Saxon times, Brighton – originally called Brighthelmston – was just a speck on the map, home to a few families of fishermen and farmers. Everything changed in 1750 after Richard Russell, a physician from Lewes, began expounding the health benefits of sea water. Visitors started flooding down from London, and that flood has never really stopped.

Brighton has always been a liberal, creative city. With historic architecture, low car ownership and a growing interest in low-impact living, it's greener than most. It was the first place in Britain to elect a Green Party MP, Caroline Lucas, and it lies within the Unesco Brighton and Lewes Downs Biosphere Reserve, created in 2014 to conserve the landscape

Highlights

- Royal Pavilion
- Brighton Seafront
- The Lanes
- North Laine
- Brighton Museum and Art Gallery
- Brighton Dome

and develop an ecologically sustainable society and economy. You'll find evidence of this everywhere, from cycle and bus lanes to eco-friendly businesses.

BRIGHTON SEAFRONT

Start your tour at **The Grand ❶** on King's Road. If you've arrived by train, head straight downhill, following the

Hire a Bike

Parking can be pricey in green-thinking Brighton. The speed limits and one-way systems are merciless, too, so it makes a lot of sense to travel on two wheels instead. A public bike hire scheme is in the pipeline; for now, try Brighton Cycle Hire (tel: 01273-571 555; www.brightoncyclehire.co.uk) under the station, or Brighton Beach Bikes (tel: 07917-753 794; www.brightonsports.co.uk) near the pier, then feel like a local as you pedal around.

sound of seagulls and the scent of the salty breeze. Queen's Road leads you down to the Jubilee Clock Tower (see page 40); from here, continue along West Street, passing the early Victorian **St Paul's Church**, and turn right at the end.

Lording it over the seafront, The Grand is a huge white wedding cake of a hotel. It hosts celebrations all year round and provides lodgings for politicians during the autumn party conference season: it was here, in 1984, that the IRA almost succeeded in assassinating Margaret Thatcher. Built in the 1860s in a style inspired by monumental Italian architecture, the building was impressive from the start; its lift was the first to be installed outside London.

Its sea views are hard to beat. **Brighton Beach ❷**, a nine-mile (14km) stretch of wave-washed pebbles, is in many ways the city's raison d'être. Though not as soft underfoot as the dunes at West Wittering or as pretty as Eastbourne's Victorian promenade, it's the pride and joy of this part of Sussex. Like a lively public park, sports arena and festival site rolled into one, this is the ultimate ur-

ban meeting place – it welcomes all comers and there's always something going on.

The Lower Promenade

If you gazed down from King's Road in Regency and Victorian times, you'd see rows of bathing machines – little cabins on wheels – beside the lower promenade. These days, the 0.75-mile (1.2km) path from the **West Pier Arches** near **Brighton i360** (see page 43) to **Brighton Pier** is lined with cafés, bars and shops, from the arty and quirky to the supremely tacky. By day, it's family-friendly, with live events to keep everyone entertained; after dark, the mood hots up when classic nightspots kick into action.

The **Fishing Quarter**, around half way along, has clinker boats and tackle on display, a reminder that in its earliest days, the shore was a mackerel-fishing settlement. The industry has dwindled but **Brighton Fishing Museum ❸** (tel: 01273-723 064; www.brightonfishingmuseum.org.uk; daily 11am–5pm) conjures vivid memories of the past through artefacts

The ornate facade of The Grand on King's Road.

Public Art in Brighton

Brighton is proud of its artistic heritage, with new site-specific installations appearing from time to time. Famous examples on the seafront include *Passacaglia* by Charles Hadcock, a dynamic curve of recycled cast iron, and the quietly subversive *Kiss Wall* by Bruce Williams, a set of six photographs reproduced by drilling dots into aluminium. For recent additions to the urban landscape, explore the North Laine and New England Quarter, epicentre of the street art scene.

The West Pier Arches, part of the Artists' Quarter.

and recordings of sea shanties. Outside, you can snack on crab or kipper sandwiches from Jack and Linda Mills Traditional Fish Smokers.

The part of the beach near the pier and the jaunty Victorian carousel is always the busiest; in summer, it can feel as if the whole world is holidaying here. The **Artists' Quarter ❹**, a clutch of seaside studios and gallery shops in the seafront arches, adds a splash of colour; the resident painters, photographers and sculptors are often around and happy to chat.

BRIGHTON PIER

For great views, candy floss and old-fashioned fun, head for **Brighton Pier ❺**, which has been drawing the crowds since 1899. In its early days it was called the Palace Pier, and had a bandstand, winter garden, waxworks and freak shows.

The pier reinvents itself every so often but it still has plenty of giggle-making rides and quirky side shows – you can test your mettle on vintage-style dodgems or scare yourself silly in the Horror Hotel, hook a duck for a prize or cheer on the contestants in the Dolphin Derby game.

Before it was built, the pier had a predecessor, the Chain Pier, which looked like four suspension bridges joined end to end. It served both as a promenade, with kiosks manned by fortune tellers, silhouette artists and souvenir sellers, and as a landing stage for passenger ships. However, it proved vulnerable to lightning and gales, and when Newhaven took over Brighton's role as a cross-channel port it gradually became a white elephant. Finally, after a great storm battered it in 1896, the town

Brighton From The Pier

The Victorians loved to promenade on their piers, enjoying the vista and the healthy sea air without the bother of getting in a boat. The view from Brighton Pier is still magnificent, with the seafront terraces rising like a cliff beyond the broad ribbon of beach. In the 1800s, when mixed-gender bathing was frowned upon, you'd have seen ladies in the water to the east and gentlemen to the west, but only at designated bathing times.

decided it was damaged beyond repair. You can sometimes still see the stumps of its oak foundations just east of Brighton Pier when the tide is very low.

SEA LIFE CENTRE

Claiming to be the oldest operating aquarium in the world, **Sea Life**

Brighton ❻ (tel: 01273-604 234; www.visitsealife.com/brighton; daily 10am–5pm), just east of the pier, first opened its doors in 1872. Originally, it was a menagerie; it switched its focus to marine life in 1929.

While much of its original, elegant vaulted architecture survives, the displays have come a long way since Vic-

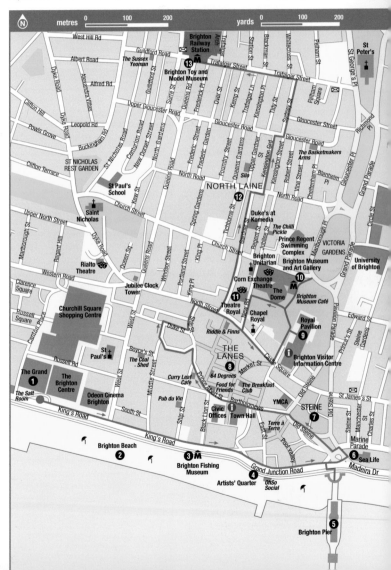

torian times. Like every marine zoo worth its salt, it has a variety of imaginatively designed tanks including one with a transparent tunnel you can walk through while sharks, turtles and tropical fish cruise overhead. There's also a nifty glass-bottomed boat which allows you to look straight down onto your new-found fishy friends from above.

Young dinosaur fans will love the Jurassic Seas exhibit, containing prehistoric creatures that are still around today. If your kids are passionate about the oceans, you can sign them up to be a keeper for a day.

Like the other Sea Life centres dotted around the world, Sea Life Brighton has a strong conservation ethic. Its staff run a pioneering seahorse breeding programme, operate a wildlife rescue service and work to raise awareness of critical issues affecting the marine environment.

THE STEINE

The string of grassy squares beside Old Steine and Grand Parade, inland from Brighton Pier, follow the valley of Brighton's underground river, the Wellesbourne, which used to flow out to sea at Pool Valley, now the coach station.

For centuries, the fishermen of Brighthelmston hauled their boats up onto the **Steine** ❼ in bad weather and spread out their nets and ropes to dry. Elegant residents appreciated this sheltered spot, too, and mansions sprang up in the late 1700s and early 1800s; some, such as 26 Old Steine, bear the trademark shell and ammonite motifs of master architect Amon Henry Wilds.

Steine House at 55 Old Steine was built for Maria Fitzherbert (see page 22), the unofficial wife of George, the Prince Regent, later George IV. She lived here from 1804 until her death in 1837, at the age of eighty. It overlooks the Victoria Fountain which, with its odd trio of dolphin-like sea creatures, was installed in 1846. The surrounding garden comes alive in May, when it hosts pop-up venues and bars for the Brighton Festival Fringe.

Old Steine and Victoria Fountain.

Jewellery shops in The Lanes.

THE LANES

Next, duck down the alley called Avenue to explore **The Lanes ❽**. There are strong echoes of Brighton's fishing-village past in this romantic quarter of medieval-style streets and twittens (passages). While many of the buildings are 18th-century, the thoroughfares they stand on, bordered by East Street, North Street and West Street, date back to the 16th-century.

In the 1970s and '80s, The Lanes were an antique shopper's treasure trove, full of old-fashioned sellers of jewellery, furniture, china and glass. Most of these dealers have since decamped to Kemptown and Lewes, but with cosy little cafés, bars, restaurants and boutiques taking their place, the quarter is still popular. Attractive shops and imaginative ethnic and vegetarian eateries can be found here,

Regency Architecture

Brighton's early 19th-century architecture outclasses any other British city outside London. Fittingly, it's named after Brighton-mad George IV, who was Prince Regent from 1811 to 1820. Grand terraced mansion buildings with tall windows and delicate neoclassical details first appeared in Brighton in the late 1790s; some of the prettiest have curved frontages and canopied balconies. They were all the rage until the 1850s, when a chunkier Victorian style took over.

Earthship Brighton

Brighton is home to the UK's first Low Carbon Trust Earthship (tel: 01273-766 601; www.lowcarbon.co.uk), an environmental education centre in Stanmer Park, on the northern edge of the city. It's an excellent example of a low-waste, low-carbon, off-grid building, constructed using recycled materials such as old car tyres. Courses are held here and staff run tours lasting 60–90 minutes around once a month, typically on a Sunday.

The Cricketers pub.

and you'll often see couples gazing longingly at vintage engagement rings in the remaining jewellers' windows.

Martha Gunn, Queen of the Dippers, lived on East Street from the mid-1700s. Famously burly, she was the most respected of the women whose job it was to assist genteel ladies out of their bathing machines then dunk them in the sea.

The Cricketers on Black Lion Street is a Victorian pub that likes to call itself Brighton's oldest boozer since there's been an inn here since 1545. Its predecessor was called the Laste and Fishcart, a laste being a measure of 10,000 herrings. On Duke Street, a Regency chapel, commissioned in 1817 by Thomas Read Kemp (see page 36), is now a contemporary art space, **Fabrica** (tel: 01273-778 646; www.fabrica.org.uk), hosting challenging installations. The old **Hippodrome** on Middle Street, formerly a circus, theatre and bingo hall, is now earmarked for reinvention as a live music venue.

ROYAL PAVILION

Make your way out of The Lanes onto North Street, then head east to the **Royal Pavilion** ❾ (tel: 030-0029

0290; www.brightonmuseums.org.uk/royalpavilion; daily Apr–Sept 9.30am–5.45pm, Oct–Mar 10am–5.15pm; audio guides for adults and children available). It stands on the site of a modest house that George, the son of King George III, rented in the mid-1780s. With a growing reputation for seawater therapy, Brighton had become decidedly fashionable; this suited the luxury-loving Prince of Wales perfectly.

He hired the architect Henry Holland to expand the house into a villa called the Marine Pavilion, furnished with chinoiserie. Later, as Prince Re-

Maria Fitzherbert

George, Prince of Wales, helped turned Brighton into one of Europe's most desirable towns. His marriage in 1785 to Maria Fitzherbert, a well-off widow from Shropshire, was officially secret, since it was illegal for a royal heir to marry a Catholic, but nonetheless the pair entertained lavishly in Brighton. When their relationship hit the rocks, George mortgaged the Pavilion to provide Maria with an income of £6,000.

gent, he commissioned John Nash to transform it completely, giving Brighton an icon unlike any other. Topped with Indian-style cast iron domes and minarets, the flamboyant design was finally completed in 1823, by which time the Regent had become King George IV.

George's successor, William IV, often spent time here but Queen Victoria, who felt uncomfortably exposed in Brighton and didn't share her uncle's extravagant tastes, decided to sell the Pavilion to the town, making it the only royal palace in Britain which is neither owned by the crown nor by the state. Daring in its day, it's so distinctive that the city council uses it as their logo.

Music Room, Banqueting Room and Kitchen

While the exterior of the Pavilion takes its cues from India, the interior is stuffed with Chinese-style excesses – rich fabrics, chic furniture and hand-painted embellishments. George inherited a love of chinoiserie from his mother, Queen Charlotte, and was an avid art collector. However, neither he nor his designers had ever travelled to the Far East, so there's a fantastical tone to the decor.

The most impressive rooms are found on the ground floor. The **Music Room**, which is exquisitely ornate, is lit by nine chandeliers shaped like parasols. The room was just large enough to hold a 70-piece orchestra including an organist. George, who liked to live in the public eye and share his enjoyment, would make sure the windows were flung open during concerts so that the music reached people promenading on the Steine.

The **Banqueting Room** is always laid for a 19th-century feast. Its crystal chandelier hangs from the claws of a dragon and its silver gilt is the most important collection of its kind. Beyond, the **Great Kitchen** is as big as a ballroom, with eccentric, palm-tree shaped pillars and a 500-piece copper batterie de cuisine. Its vast ranges, roasting spits and hot water supply were state of the art.

ROYAL PAVILION GARDENS

The **Royal Pavilion Gardens** are green in summer and magical in winter, when a Christmassy ice skating

The Royal Pavilion.

Brighton Museum and Art Gallery.

rink operates on the lawn between the Pavilion and the Steine. The main public garden on New Road is laid out in Regency style, with curving paths and ornamental flowering shrubs.

Brighton Museum and Art Gallery

In an ornate building that once housed royal servants, the **Brighton Museum and Art Gallery** ⑩ (tel: 030-0029 0290; www.brighton museums.org.uk/brighton; Tue–Sun 10am–5pm) in the Pavilion Gardens is an airy, high-ceilinged space devoted to 19th- and 20th-century fashion, style, furniture, design and performing arts. It also has an illuminating section exploring local history and popular culture through old photos, artefacts and oral accounts. There's a display on the Mods and Rockers and references to Brighton as a gay and lesbian capital and a dirty weekend getaway.

Talks and exhibitions are held here from time to time, and there's an attractive café on the balcony over the 20th-century Art and Design Gallery.

Brighton Dome and Theatre Royal

Next door, the **Brighton Dome** (tel: 01273-709 709; www.brighton dome.org), now the city's principal concert hall, continues the architectural themes of the Pavilion. It's a drum-shaped building with a dome that was one of the biggest in the world when it was completed in 1808. Built at huge expense as the Prince of Wales' stables, it could house 62 horses along with their grooms and farriers, and was converted to a concert hall in 1935. It's now part of a performance and exhibition complex that also contains the **Corn Exchange** and **Pavilion Theatre**.

On New Road, Brighton's early 19th-century **Theatre Royal** ⑪ (tel: 0844-871 7650; www.atgtickets.com) shows West End plays. Great actors and dancers including Laurence Olivier, John Gielgud, Margot Fonteyn and

Best Ice Cream in Town

If your kids are ice cream conoisseurs, make for Gelato Gusto (2 Gardner Street; www.gelatogusto. com) in the North Laine, which has scrumptious flavours such as jaffa cake and lemon meringue pie. Cloud 9 (15 Brighton Place; www.cloud9brighton.co.uk) in The Lanes, inventor of the rainbow cake, also serves fabulous ice cream, waffles and milk shakes, while Boho Gelato (Pool Valley; www.bohogelato.couk) has turned handmade gelato into an art form.

Judi Dench have appeared here over the years.

NORTH LAINE

Head back to North Street then turn up Bond Street to enter the **North Laine** ⑫. Not to be confused with The Lanes, this quintessentially Brightonian quarter of Victorian terraced cottages and bohemian cafés, pubs and performance venues is the living, breathing embodiment of the city's independent-minded, fun-loving side. It has the city's best cin-

ema, **Duke's at Komedia** (44 Gardner Street; www.picturehouses.com), and is a fantastic place to shop.

In 1976, when it was the norm to build concrete flats, office blocks and flyovers in British cities, the entire district was in danger of demolition. However, local planning director Ken Fines convinced Brighton Council that it should be made a conservation area, naming it North Laine after the open field on which it was originally built.

Today it's always teeming with young hipsters in artfully mismatched clothes, particularly on sunny weekends when shoppers regroup and revive at the outdoor tables of cafés and pubs. Its principal streets, Bond Street, Gardner Street, Kensington Gardens and Sydney Street, connect North Street to Trafalgar Street, immediately east of the station. Its main square is on Jubilee Street, outside the modern Jubilee Library.

Independent shops and galleries

Cool galleries and street art – including a reproduction of Brighton's famous Banksy on Frederick Place – help give the North Laine its dis-

North Laine.

tinctive character. **Ink_d Gallery and Studio** (96 North Road; www.ink-d.co.uk) represents cutting edge contemporary and urban creatives, while **Gallery 40** (40 Gloucester Road; www.gallery40.co.uk) shows work by emerging artists from Brighton University. Found-object sculptor Chris Macdonald sells his work from **Sculpture24** (24 Foundry Street; www.chrismacdonaldsculptor.com), which doubles as his workshop and home. For beautiful, affordable paintings and gifts by other local designers and craftworkers, try the **IO Gallery** (39 Sydney Street; www.iogallery.co.uk).

Vintage shopping is another North Laine speciality, with masses of oddments on offer in **Snooper's Paradise** (7–8 Kensington Gardens; www.snoopersattic.co.uk) upcycled clothing in **Beyond Retro** (42 Vine Street; www.beyondretro.com) and cult retro gear in **Dirty Harry** (6 Sydney Street; www.dirtyharryltd.com) and **To Be Worn Again** (24 Sydney Street; www.tobewornagain.co.uk).

Other one-off shops worth checking out are **Magazine Brighton** (22 Trafalgar Street; www.magazinebrighton.com) for independent magazines and **Resident** (28 Kensington Gardens; www.resident-music.com) for rare vinyl records.

Street art on Kensington Street.

The curved glass and iron roof of Brighton Station.

BRIGHTON TOY MUSEUM AND STATION

On the northern edge of the North Laine, tucked under the arches beneath the station, is **Brighton Toy and Model Museum** ⑬ (Trafalgar Street tel: 01273-749 494; www.

brightontoymuseum.co.uk; Tue–Fri 10am–5pm, Sat 11am–5pm). Aimed at nostalgic adults as well as children, it has over 10,000 exhibits. Appropriately enough, given its location, model railways are its forte. The owner, an avid collector, has also assembled teddy bears, puppets, dolls and games, some over a century old.

By the 1830s, more than 100,000 visitors were travelling to Brighton by coach each year, and when the railway line from London to **Brighton Station** opened in 1841, the town's status as a seaside resort was firmly assured.

Brighton resident Laurence Olivier was one of the many fans of the Brighton Belle, a 1930s electric train which ran daily from Victoria until 1972; it was so luxurious that the writer Keith Waterhouse described it as "the Palace of Versailles pulled out into a string of sausages". Enthusiasts are now working to get the Brighton Belle, fully restored, back on the rails.

Ethical Shopping

Anita Roddick launched her first ever Body Shop in the North Laine and the area is still a hub of ethical and alternative trading. Try Vegetarian Shoes (12 Gardner Street; www.vegetarian-shoes. co.uk) for animal-friendly fabric footwear, Infinity Foods (25 North Road; www.infinityfoods.co.uk) for organic treats or Retail Therapy (101 Gloucester Road; www.retailtherapy. uk.com) for herbal remedies. Bonsai-Ko (www.bonsai-ko.co.uk) has been selling bonsai trees from a suitably small shop at 24 Sydney Street for over 25 years.

Eating Out

64 Degrees
53 Meeting House Lane; tel: 01273-770 115; www.64degrees.co.uk; daily noon–3pm and 6–9.45pm.
This strikingly modern eatery is a favourite among Brighton foodies. Named after the perfect temperature at which to cook an egg, its chefs prepare inventive dishes with scientific precision in the open kitchen. Portions are small; you order a selection to nibble and share. ££

The Basketmakers Arms
12 Gloucester Road; tel: 01273-689 006; www. basket-makers-brighton. co.uk; food served daily noon–9pm.
Attracting a mix of students, visitors and locals who have been drinking here for decades, this North Laine pub serves some of the best kept real ale in the city. There's a no-nonsense menu of organic fare and a refreshingly traditional atmosphere. £

The Breakfast Club
16–17 Market Street; tel: 01273-947 080; www.thebreakfastclubcafes. com; Mon–Wed 8am–11pm, Thu–Sat 8am–11.30pm, Sun 8am–10.30pm.
Style-conscious Brighton folk have lapped up The Breakfast Club's first foray out of London. Its trademarks are a quirky '70s theme and a huge selection of breakfast specials, many available all day, "because it's always breakfast time somewhere in the world". £

Brighton Museum Café
Royal Pavilion Gardens; tel: 03000-290 900; www.brightonmuseums.org. uk; Tue–Sun 10am–4.30pm.
Museum visitors can enjoy treats such as artichoke and cress quiche, South Coast fish pie or treacle tart with clotted cream at this licensed café in the stylish surroundings of the 20th-century Art and Design Gallery. £

The Chilli Pickle
17 Jubilee Street; tel: 01273-900 383; www.thechillipickle.com; daily noon–3pm and 6–10.30pm.
This award-winning independent restaurant offers flavoursome cuisine inspired by Indian street food. As you'd expect, the menu includes some great vegetarian dishes. The owners often jet off to India for fresh inspiration. £££

The Coal Shed
8 Boyce's Street; tel: 01273-322 998; www.coalshed-restaurant.co.uk; Mon–Thu noon–4pm and 6–10pm, Fri–Sat noon–4pm and 6–10.30pm, Sun noon–4pm and 6–9.30pm.
Famous for its succulent steak – sold by the cut and the weight, and chargrilled at high temperatures for perfect results – this acclaimed bistro also serves oysters and sharing plates. There's a great value weekday lunch and pre-theatre menu. If you're vegetarian, check in advance that there's something to suit. £££

Curry Leaf Café
60 Ship Street; tel: 01273-207 070; www.curryleafcafe.com; Mon–Sat noon–3pm and 6–10.30pm, Sun noon–3.30 and 6–10pm.
Run by an Indian chef who used to work at The Chilli Pickle (see above), this little backstreet eatery offers a fresh interpretation of Indian street food. Every dish bursts with colourful ingredients and around half the menu is vegetarian. £

Food for Friends
17–18 Prince Albert Street; tel: 01273-202 310; www.foodforfriends. com; Mon–Thu noon–10pm, Fri–Sat noon–10.30pm, Sun noon–10pm.
In the heart of the Lanes, this vegetarian eatery has had a few makeovers since it opened in 1981, but it never falls out of favour. These

days it's a sophisticated modern restaurant creating imaginative dishes inspired by the flavours of the Middle East, North Africa and the Mediterranean. ££

OhSo Social

250A King's Road Arches; tel: 01273-746 067; www.ohsobrighton.co.uk; daily 9am–2am.

There are fewer alfresco restaurants on Brighton beach than you might expect, so the terrace at OhSo Social is always busy on sunny days. In a prime spot near the Lanes and Brighton Pier, it serves family-friendly breakfasts and grills by day and party zone cocktails and beers after dark. ££

Pub du Vin

7 Ship Street; tel: 01273-718 588; www. hotelduvin.com; daily noon–11pm.

In a Georgian building adjacent to Brighton's Hotel du Vin, this is the celebrated hotel chain's stylish twist on a traditional English pub. It serves real ale in pewter tankards and offers gourmet versions of old-fashioned favourites such as steak and kidney pie, beer-battered fish and chips and Scotch eggs. ££

Riddle and Finns

139 Kings Road Arches; tel: 01273-821 218; www.riddleandfinns.co.uk; daily noon–9pm.

This relaxed beach restaurant is an offshoot of Riddle and Finns in the Lanes, Brighton's highly successful champagne, oyster and seafood bar, with an equally tempting menu. To get one of the prized tables in the upstairs window, book in advance; there's also a terrace to enjoy in warm weather. £££

The Sussex Yeoman

7 Guildford Road; tel: 01273-327 985; www.thesussexyeoman.com; food served Mon–Thu noon–3pm

and 6–10pm, Fri–Sat noon–10pm, Sun noon–7pm.

Arguably the best gastropub in central Brighton, The Sussex Yeoman prides itself on its ethically sourced ingredients. Top quality steak, sausages and grilled mackerel often appear on the menu and the Sunday roast is legendary. It's also handily close to the station. £

The Salt Room

106 King's Road; tel: 01273-929 488; www.saltroom-restaurant.co.uk; Mon–Thu noon–4pm and 6–10pm, Fri–Sat noon–4pm and 6–10.30pm, Sun noon–4pm and 6–9.30pm.

Like its sister restaurant, The Coal Shed (see above), this smart seafront eatery has perfected the art of chargrill cooking, but with a focus on fish, from bream with clams and samphire to fish burgers. Sunday lunch is a convivial affair, with roasts served as a sharing platter. £££

Silo

39 Upper Gardner Street; tel: 01273-674 259; www.silobrighton.com; Mon–Wed 8.30am–5pm, Thu–Sat 8.30am–8.30pm, Sun 10am–5pm.

Britain's first zero-waste restaurant received a heartfelt welcome from eco-minded Brightonians when it opened in 2015. It sources all its fresh ingredients locally and composts leftovers on site. The food is modern, fresh and wholesome. £

Terre à Terre

71 East Street; tel: 01273-729 051; www.terreaterre.co.uk; Mon–Fri noon–10.30pm, Sat 11am–11pm, Sun 11am–10pm.

Brighton's most celebrated vegetarian restaurant offers elaborately conceived and imaginatively described dishes. It has more competition than it used to, but it still pulls in the accolades. £££

Feature

Brighton Festival

Brighton Festival

Each May around half a million people attend events across Brighton and Hove as part of the annual Brighton Festival

England's largest arts festival originated as a student rag week with the aim of fundraising money for the arts. The first festival took place in 1967 and featured performers such as Laurence Olivier, Anthony Hopkins and violinist Yehudi Menuhin. Ian Hunter, Artistic Director 1967–83, described it as an event 'where the serious and the apparently flippant ride side by side'. Artists such as Ella Fitzgerald, Count Basie, Elvis Costello, Courtney Pine – and, more recently, Mercury Prize nominee Kate Tempest – have performed here, along with orchestras and dance troupes from around the world. Countless comedians and writers, from Eddie Izzard to Alan Bennett and Gore Vidal, have entertained and inspired audiences.

Marking its 50th anniversary in 2016, today's festival offers a varied programme of music, theatre, dance, visual art, film, literature and circus performances. Alongside plays at the Theatre Royal, concerts at Brighton Dome and classical music performances in the Royal Pavilion's sumptuous Music Room, a range of less conventional venues, including pubs, churches and parks, hosts everything from stand-up comedy to debates on culture and politics.

Concert at the Dome; Children's Parade; street theatre in the Pavilion Gardens.

Going Out in Brighton

Brighton Centre Brighton's leading venue for big name bands and comedians. www.brightoncentre.co.uk

Brighton Dome, Corn Exchange and **Studio Theatre** Once the Prince Regent's stables, this flexible performance space is the hub of the Brighton Festival each May. www.brightondome.org

Concorde 2 This grungey music venue has hosted some of the greats of the indie music scene, from Jarvis Cocker to local lad Fatboy Slim. www.concorde2.co.uk

Duke of York's and **Duke's at Komedia** Two arthouse cinemas: a splendid 1920s purpose-built picture house at Preston Circus and a luxurious venue in the North Laine. www.picturehouses.com

Komedia Famous for comedy, Komedia also offers indie bands, and retro and club nights. www.komedia.co.uk

Patterns Wildly popular recent addition to the club scene, brimming with original ideas. www.patternsbrighton.com

Proud Cabaret Distinctly different, this is a cabaret club with dinner and burlesque entertainers. www.proudcabaretbrighton.com

Revenge At the heart of Brighton's gay village, Revenge is all about bright lights, big beats and outrageous dressing up.

Shooshh One of the swankiest of the clubs under the arches on Brighton Beach. www.brighton.shooshh.com

Theatre Royal Atmospheric, 200-year-old venue for West End style shows. www.atgtickets.com

In recent years, a guest artistic director has been invited to curate the festival, often following a designated theme. Past directors include such luminaries as sculptor Anish Kapoor, writer Ali Smith and the Burmese democracy leader Aung San Suu Kyi.

At the start of the festival thousands of school children parade through the city's streets in colourful costumes and there are plays, workshops and circus performances aplenty to enthral young children.

Running alongside the main festival, Brighton Fringe promotes local talent, from newcomers to established acts. Tickets for many shows are free.

George Street in Kemptown.

Tour 2

East Brighton and Rottingdean

Get to know a vibrant part of Brighton by taking this 8-mile (13km) tour of Kemptown and Rottingdean on foot, by vintage railway and by bus

When George the Prince Regent and his entourage made Brighton fashionable in the late 1700s, the breezy cliffs east of the Royal Pavilion quickly became the place to be. Terraced mansions popped up and St James's Street grew from a country track into a high-class shopping street which, in 1826, a visitor from London described as 'the Bond Street of Brighton'.

St James's Street is far less posh these days, but it leads to some of 21st-century Brighton's coolest neighbourhoods. In Kemptown Village, bohemian pubs, cafés and bric-a-brac shops are framed by neat streets of Regency and Victorian houses, while, further east, the Kemp Town Estate is spacious and grand. The coastal village of Rottingdean is also worth visiting for its arty atmosphere and Kipling connections.

Highlights

- Kemp Town Estate
- Queen's Park
- Kemptown Village
- Volk's Electric Railway
- Kipling Gardens, Rottingdean

QUEEN'S PARK

The first section of this tour is a 3-mile (5km) walk around Queen's Park and Kemptown, including the Kemp Town Estate.

Ringed by avenues of desirable Victorian houses, **Queen's Park ❶** is one of the city's largest green spaces. Created in the 1820s, it was named after Queen Adelaide in 1836 and became a public park in 1890. Its duck pond, lawns, shady trees, playground and wilderness area are hugely popular with families.

The curious tower at the north end is known as the Pepper Pot. Designed in 1830 by Sir Charles Barry, architect of the House of Commons and Brighton's Royal Sussex County Hospital, it housed a steam engine that pumped water to a grand Italianate villa which once stood here.

KEMPTOWN VILLAGE

From Queen's Park, walk south down Egremont Place, then cross Eastern Road and continue down Upper Rock Gardens, a pleasant Victorian street with sparkling sea views on a fine day. At **St Mary's Church** ❷, a large 1870s red brick church, turn east into St James's Street, which leads into Upper St James's Street. This is the start of **Kemptown Village**, home to quirky shops and interesting places to eat and drink. The street changes name to Bristol Road

A flock of geese in Queens Park, one of the city's largest green spaces.

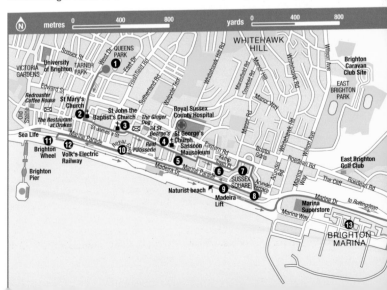

New Steine.

and St George's Road as you continue east.

On Bristol Road, **St John the Baptist's Church** ❸ was Brighton's first Roman Catholic church to be built in Brighton. Completed in 1835, it was funded by Maria Fitzherbert (see page 22), the secret first wife of the Prince Regent, and is her burial place. Further east, there are fine sea views from **Portland Place**, whose stucco-fronted mansions offer a taste of what's to come in the Kemp Town Estate. Just beyond Abbey Road – named after a local brewing family whose maltings stood nearby – is **St George's Church** ❹. With clean, elegant neoclassical lines and an airy interior, it's an attractive parish church that's often used for concerts.

Nearby, on Paston Place, is an oddity – the **Sassoon Mausoleum** ❺, currently a nightclub, Proud Cabaret. Like an outpost of the Royal Pavilion, it's topped with a dome. Sir Albert Sassoon, a well-connected Iraqi Jew who made a fortune in India then retired to Kemptown, commissioned it in 1892. He and his son Edward were interred there after they died – Albert in 1896 and Edward in 1912 – but his family eventually decided their remains should be moved to the Willesden Jewish Cemetery in London.

Gay Brighton

The area of eastern Brighton immediately northeast of Brighton Pier is the city's unofficial LGBT village. This is where you'll find Brighton's top gay clubs, Revenge (32 Old Steine; www.revenge.co.uk) and Legends (31 Marine Parade; www.legendsbrighton.com). They're always buzzing, especially during Pride (www.brighton-pride.org) in August, which is Britain's biggest, with an upbeat parade through town and a festival at Preston Park. The west end of St James's Street is dotted with LGBT bars and boutiques; it can feel raffish but in true Brighton style it has some beautiful Regency detailing and an eclectic mix of cafés, pubs and shops with broad appeal. The bronze sculpture in New Steine, a garden square with sea views, is an Aids memorial.

Antiques and bric-a-brac

These days, Kemptown easily trumps The Lanes as a hotspot for vintage oddments. There's a string of interesting shops in Kemptown Village, including Brighton Flea Market at 31A Upper St James's Street and Kemp Town Trading Post at 28 St George's Road.

KEMP TOWN ESTATE

Turn north along Eaton Place, east along Chesham Road, south along Chichester Place and then east into Rock Grove. You're now in the **Kemp Town Estate**, built when this area was still open downland. The smart flint cottages of **Kemp Town Place**  were the mews for the seafront mansions of **Chichester Terrace**. Bear north past the Busby and Wilds pub on Rock Street and east along Eastern Road to enter the jewel

Elegant Lewes Crescent, part of the Kemp Town Estate.

of the estate, **Sussex Square** ❼, its white stucco and brick facades linked to the seafront by the elegant curves of **Lewes Crescent**. The central gardens are not open to the public, but the square is worth visiting for the architecture alone.

Thomas Read Kemp, who conceived the estate in 1823 and financed its early stages, lived at 22 Sussex Square from 1828 to 1837, while he

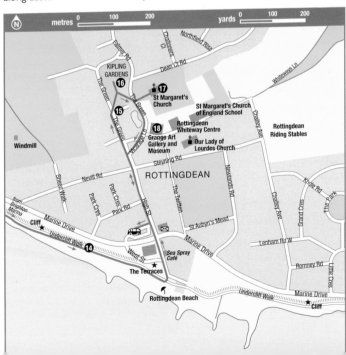

Brighton Beach and the Brighton Wheel.

Kemptown's Architects

In 1823, local politician Thomas Read Kemp hired architects Charles Busby, Amon Wilds and his son Amon Henry Wilds to develop the Kemp Town Estate. The project, which took over 30 years, was a gamble which brought Kemp financial ruin. Busby, Wilds and Wilds created much of Brighton's distinguished Regency architecture, including St George's Church (designed in 1824) and Brunswick Square (see page 45). Fans of Gothic Revival will be impressed by Brighton College, Sussex's first public school, whose main buildings on Eastern Road were designed in the 1840s by Sir George Gilbert Scott, architect of London's Albert Memorial and St Pancras Hotel, and extended in the 1880s by Sir Thomas Graham Jackson, who created Oxford's Bridge of Sighs. The last part of Jackson's design, a grand gatehouse clocktower, was finally slotted into place in 2014.

was MP for Lewes, after which he fled to France to escape his creditors. The estate's master builder, Thomas Cubitt, lived at 13 Lewes Crescent from 1846 to 1855, the year construction was complete.

The first section was **Arundel Terrace ⑧**, a cliff-like row of seafront mansions with Corinthian columns. The other terraces are equally handsome, with tall Regency windows and cast iron balconies.

MARINE PARADE AND MADEIRA DRIVE

Next, enjoy a 1.5-mile (2.5km) walk along the seafront. In the 19th century, **Marine Parade** at the top of East Cliff and **Madeira Drive** at the foot were a place to be seen. These days, Madeira Drive acts as a showground for vintage car rallies, speed trials and other events on many summer weekends.

If you wish, you can drop down from Marine Parade via Duke's Mound, the road opposite Chichester Terrace. Brighton's famous **Naturist Beach** is near here, shielded by

brightonwheel.com; daily 10am–9pm, Fri–Sat until 11pm), an observation wheel; near its foot is the tiny terminus of **Volk's Electric Railway** 12 (www.volkselectricrailway.co.uk; Easter–Sept Tue–Thu 10.15am–5pm, Mon and Fri 11.15am–5pm, Sat–Sun 10.15am–6pm). Dating back to 1883, it's the oldest narrow gauge electric railway in Britain. Its inventor, Magnus Volk, a clockmaker's son, also installed electric light in the Royal Pavilion and designed the original mechanism for the Clock Tower's time-ball (see page 40). Take a seat in one of the open-sided carriages and enjoy the sea views as it trundles the 1.2 miles (2km) to Black Rock, just west of the marina; alternatively, catch a bus to the marina from Marine Parade.

When **Brighton Marina** 13 (tel: 01273-693 636; www.brightonmarina.co.uk) was built, mostly of concrete, in the 1970s, it was the largest of its type in Europe, and thanks to a controversial new development it's gradually expanding upwards. Its unremarkable

a bank of pebbles. Alternatively, you can descend via one of the flights of steps, or via the **Madeira Lift** 9 (Apr–Sept), in a quirky booth with a weathervane opposite Marine Square. Built in 1890, the original was operated by a hydraulic pump.

If you remain up on Marine Parade, there's splendid Regency architecture to appreciate. **Royal Crescent** 10, the earliest of Brighton's grand seafront terraces, is a highlight. Designed in 1798, it's clad in black mathematical tiles: brick-shaped, weather-resistant glazed tiles which were very fashionable in Brighton and Lewes. From 1961 to 1979, Sir Laurence Olivier and his wife Joan Plowright lived at No. 4, commuting to the Chichester Festival Theatre and, on the Brighton Belle train, to the National Theatre in London.

VOLK'S ELECTRIC RAILWAY

If you're not already down on Madeira Drive, descend via the steps opposite Rock Place to a busy stretch of seaside, with places to grab a drink or an ice cream.

You can't miss the **Brighton Wheel** 11 (tel: 01273-722 822; www.

Volk's Electric Railway runs along the seafront.

Kemptown Beach

On Madeira Drive, there's a fun little playground, mini golf and Yellowave Beachsports (www.yellowave.co.uk), with beach volleyball courts, a sandy play area and a family-friendly café. Concorde 2 (www.concorde2.co.uk) is a student favourite – originally the waiting room for the Madeira Lift, this Victorian pavilion is now a cherished indie music venue.

shops, restaurants and entertainment facilities have always felt out of character for Brighton but its Sunday morning car boot sale is lively and its harbour is the launch point for boat trips.

ROTTINGDEAN

On a bright day, it's an invigorating 2.5-mile (4km) walk along the **Undercliff Path ⑭** from Brighton Marina to **Rottingdean**'s popular little pebble beach. If you'd prefer to travel by bus (Nos 27 or 47 Mon–Sat; 27, 14B or 57 Sun), hop on by McDonalds and alight at the White Horse pub. Buses to and from central Brighton stop here every few minutes, too.

Rottingdean's narrow High Street leads northwest to **The Green ⑮**.

It's picturesque, with a Saxon duck pond which would have been used for everything from watering horses to wheel-washing and firefighting, crucial in the days of muddy tracks and thatched roofs.

North of the pond are the **Kipling Gardens ⑯**, a flint-walled public park, fragrant with roses and herbs. It used to belong to the adjacent house, The Elms, which Rudyard Kipling and his family rented from 1897 to 1902 before moving to Bateman's (see page 81). It was here that Kipling began writing his *Just So Stories*. The park is well tended, with a wildflower area and beehives.

Other writers and artists have been drawn to Rottingdean over the years, including Sir Edward Burne-Jones and William Morris, who together produced stained glass windows for the flint-walled **St Margaret's Church ⑰**, opposite The Elms. In a Georgian house on the corner of Whiteway Lane, southeast of the pond, the **Grange Art Gallery and Museum ⑱** (tel: 01273-301 004; Mon–Tue and Thu–Sun 10.30am–4.30pm) has exhibits on Burne-Jones and Kipling and displays of contemporary art. The garden, designed by Sir Edwin Lutyens, has recently been restored.

Kipling Gardens.

Eating Out

24 St George's

24 St George's Road; tel: 01273-626 060; www.24stgeorges.co.uk; Tue–Fri 5.30–10pm, Sat 12.30–10pm.

This is the restaurant which made Kemptown Village a gastronomic destination of note. The decor is sleek and the menu sumptuous, featuring modern European classics such as sea bream with paella jus or pork fillet with fermented garlic gnocchi. There's also an extensive wine list, making this a good choice for a special occasion. £££

The Ginger Dog

12–13 College Place; tel: 01273-620 990; www.thegingerdog.com; daily 11.30am–11.30pm.

You can tell this cosy restaurant used to be a neighbourhood boozer – they've even kept the bar and open fire – but the tables are now crammed with diners rather than drinkers. The cooking is sophisticated, with gorgeous flavour combinations such as pork with charred cabbage or cod with green mango. £££

Marmalade

237 Eastern Road; tel: 01273-606 138; www.cafemarmalade.co.uk; Mon–Sat 8am–6pm, Sun 9am–5pm.

West of Sussex Square, this lovely little café with a wholesome, distressed-vintage vibe is a locals' favourite. As well as scrumptious breakfasts of porridge, eggs, smoothies and pastries, it offers imaginative salads, delicious savoury tarts and sandwiches, along with retro teatime treats such as crumpets and scones. £

Real Patisserie

34 St George's Road; tel: 01273-609 655; www.realpatisserie.co.uk; Mon–Sat 7.30am–5.30pm.

Like a little corner of France transported to Kemptown, this bakery sells delectable fruit tarts, slices of quiche, hot stuffed croissants and sandwiches made from crunchy, freshly baked bread. They also do takeaway coffee. You could take your hoard down to the beach or just sit at the farmhouse table and scoff the lot. £

Redroaster Coffee House

1D St James's Street; tel: 01273-686 668; www.redroaster.co.uk; Mon–Sat 7am–7pm, Sun 8am–6.30pm.

Brighton may be flooded with excellent coffee shops but this long-standing favourite, just off the Steine, never goes out of style. Bohemian but not scruffy, it's a spacious and appealing place to relax over a cup of the house roast with a big slice of gâteau. £

The Restaurant at Drakes

43–4 Marine Parade; tel: 01273-696 934; www.therestaurantatdrakes. co.uk; daily 12.30–2pm and 7–10pm.

Downstairs at Drakes, one of Brighton's classiest boutique hotels, is this award-winning modern British restaurant, intimate enough for a special occasion. Chef Andrew Mackenzie works wonders with Sussex ingredients such as game and pork belly to create dishes which are both comforting and exciting – a winning formula. £££

Sea Spray Café

18 High Street, Rottingdean; tel: 01273-307 732; Wed–Sun 9am–5pm.

Cheerfully old-fashioned, Sea Spray is a Rottingdean institution that's been serving fluffy omelettes, home-made soup and excellent Italian-style coffee to holidaymakers and locals since the 1940s. In summer, there's also ice cream. £

View over Brunswick Square and Hove Lawns.

Tour 3

West Brighton and Hove

Enjoy glorious sea views and admire some of Britain's most impressive seafront architecture on this 4-mile (6km) urban walk

Originally separated by open countryside, Brighton and Hove gradually merged in Victorian times and became, officially, a single city in 2001. However, even now, Hove retains its own distinctive atmosphere. As you make your way west from central Brighton, the avenues and squares get wider and the pace of life seems to get gentler.

This walking tour shows you some superb Regency and early Victorian architecture. You'll explore elegant streets of mansions dotted with intricate details such as ammonites, shells and Corinthian flourishes. On the way, you'll have the chance to relax in quiet gardens and enjoy lungfuls of fresh sea air on Hove's peaceful, civilised beach.

Highlights

- Regency Square
- The Bandstand
- Brunswick Terrace
- Brunswick Square
- Regency Town House
- Hove Esplanade

JUBILEE CLOCK TOWER

Everyone who heads straight downhill from Brighton station to the beach passes the **Jubilee Clock Tower ❶** on the way. Standing at the crossroads of Queens Road, North Street and West Street, it marks the centre of the city's main commercial district, and acts as a pole for bunting, stream-

Churchill Square

The area west of the Clock Tower is Brighton's hotspot for big name high street stores. The city is famed as a retail therapy destination and its most conventional shopping mall, Churchill Square, was ahead of its time, winning an award when it opened in the 1990s. Wedged between West Street and busy Western Road, it's pleasantly airy.

ers and fairylights during festivals and the Christmas shopping season.

The tower, unveiled in 1888 to mark the first anniversary of Queen Victoria's Golden Jubilee, features mosaic portraits of Victoria, Albert and the Prince and Princess of Wales, Edward and Alexandra. The golden time-ball on top, designed by Magnus Volk (see page 37), used to rise up the spike and drop with a clang to signal the hour to passing ships. The original mechanism has been removed, however, and the modern replacement is rather erratic.

REGENCY SQUARE CONSERVATION AREA

From the Clock Tower, walk west into the plaza outside Churchill Square, and from its southwest corner make your

The Jubilee Clock Tower, where Queens Road meets North Street.

way west into **Clarence Square** ❷, an early 1800s garden square with plain facades that were added later. Next, continue south into **Russell Square** ❸, which retains far more of its original Regency character, despite the distraction of the car park on the east side. A twitten (small passage) in the southwest corner leads past the **Regency Tavern**, which retains its historic feel with an outrageously camp interior complete with twinkling chandeliers.

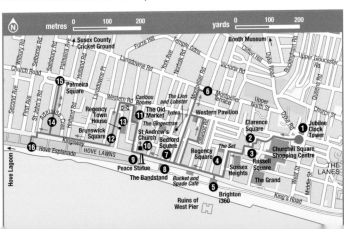

Regency Square ❹ is one of Brighton's set pieces. Before this elegant brick and stucco garden square was built, the site was used for the military camp which Jane Austen featured in *Pride and Prejudice*; it held such glamorous allure for Lydia Bennet that she dashed away there to elope with a soldier.

Construction of the square began in 1818. The developer, Joshua Hanson, set a few ground rules – each house had to have a cast iron balcony, for example – and invited private builders to take on different sections. Many houses, which were unusually large for the time, were designed by Amon Wilds and his son, Amon Henry Wilds. Effectively, this was a warm-up for the grander building projects of the Kemp Town Estate and Brunswick Town, which soon followed.

Views from Regency Square

The first residents looked out onto a landscaped garden where concerts were held, with gloriously wide, unobstructed sea views beyond. Over the years, the vista has changed enormously. The first addition was Eugenius Birch's **West Pier**, which opened in 1866. It was a supremely elegant structure, framed by the

Brighton i360

The latest addition to the Brighton skyline is the startlingly modern i360 (www.brightoni360.co.uk), an observation tower ringed by a doughnut-shaped viewing platform which ascends to 138m for views of the city, coast and Downs. Created by the team behind the London Eye, it's on the seafront opposite Regency Square. While its supporters describe it as a pier in the sky and a fitting successor to the much-loved West Pier, it has plenty of detractors who feel it's vulgar and totally inappropriate.

square, and at the peak of its popularity, between the world wars, locals and visitors alike flocked to its concert hall. Sadly, the pier fell into disrepair in the 1970s and was destroyed in the 2000s by storms and fire, leaving a picturesque ruin.

In the 1960s, the south coast's tallest residential tower, the sleekly modernist Sussex Heights, popped up east of the square, and an underground car park was built, ruining the garden. Plans are now underway for celebrity gardener Diarmuid Gavin

Regency Square.

The remains of the West Pier.

to redesign the garden, partly funded by proceeds of **Brighton i360** ❺, a new attraction which dominates the view like nothing before. It stands over 15 times taller than the impressive 1904 **Second Boer War memorial** at the south end of the square.

West of Regency Square
From the south side of Regency Square, head west along King's Road, named after King George IV, where among the 19th-century seafront buildings you'll pass a 1930s block and a couple of later additions. Bedford Towers, a 17-storey 1960s block housing flats and the Holiday Inn, hogs the old site of the Bedford Hotel, which was tragically destroyed by fire in 1964. This palatial, late-Georgian hotel had been extremely fashionable in its day; Charles Dickens wrote *Dombey and Son* during a stay there. The modern style and colour of the 14-storey, dark brick Cavendish Court caused a scandal when it went up in the 1960s; it replaced one of the few detached Regency mansions on the seafront.

If you're interested in Regency architecture, you could make a diversion up **Oriental Place**, which is lined with monumental mansions, many with decorative columns topped with ammonite motifs, the architectural trademark of Amon Henry Wilds. From here, you can explore hidden gems such as **Sillwood Road**, where a plaque at No. 11 marks the site where the artist John Constable had a studio, and **Western Terrace**, where Amon Henry Wilds built him-

The Booth Museum
Connoisseurs of Victoriana and children with an eye for the macabre will love the exhibits at the Booth Museum (194 Dyke Road; tel: 03000-290 901; www.brighton museums.org.uk/booth; Mon–Wed and Fri–Sat 10am–5pm, Sun 2–5pm), a very traditional museum that's now been updated with interactive displays. Stars of the show are Edward Booth's original collection of birds, butterflies, bugs and oddities, dating back to 1874.

The Bandstand.

self a private residence, Western Pavilion, inspired by the Royal Pavilion. For some of the best Regency villas in Brighton, continue north via Montpelier Road to wander around **Montpelier** ❻, a conservation area crammed with listed residential buildings, before returning to the seafront.

The Bandstand and Peace Statue

Bedford Square ❼ is Brighton's earliest square, designed in 1801. From here, cross King's Road to **The Bandstand** ❽, a great spot to buy an ice cream, flop into a deckchair and enjoy some seaside nostalgia. It's the sole survivor of the dozen bandstands which graced the parks and promenades of Brighton and Hove in Victorian times. They fell out of favour in the 1960s when traffic noise began to drown out the music, but this one, sometimes called The Birdcage because of its delicate ironwork, has been restored by local heritage enthusiasts and hosts free Sunday afternoon concerts in summer.

Continue west along the seafront to the bronze angel known as the **Peace Statue** ❾, a favourite landmark in peace-loving Brighton. Commemorating King Edward VII who died in 1910,

it was built, poignantly, in 1912, two years before war broke out. It stands opposite **Embassy Court**, a huge, sleek, 1930s apartment block in Modernist style, and marks the boundary between Brighton and Hove. The inscription on one side is Brighton's motto (*In Deo Fidemus*, In God We Trust), while Hove's is on the other (*Floreat Hova*, May Hove Flourish).

BRUNSWICK CONSERVATION AREA

From the Peace Statue, there are superb, sweeping views of the clotted-cream-coloured terraces of Hove's

Hove Lagoon

On the esplanade just under three miles (2km) from central Brighton, Hove Lagoon is the city's watersports training lake. Its safe waters are perfect for building or boosting skills before setting out to sea. Lagoon Sports (Kingsway; tel: 01273-424 842; www.lagoon.co.uk) offers fun classes in windsurfing and stand-up paddleboarding for kids aged eight and up, and wakeboarding for those aged 10+. There's a café and playground, too.

Sussex County Cricket

The thwack of leather on willow has been ringing around Hove since 1872 when Sussex, the world's oldest county cricket club, made Eaton Road its permanent home. The County Ground (tel: 0844-264 0202; www.sussexcricket.co.uk) hosts fixtures all season and a cracking Bonfire Night firework display.

prime conservation area, fronted by **Hove Lawns**. When it was laid out in the 1820s, **Brunswick Town** was a smart enclave, surrounded by open downland. The majestic mansions of **Brunswick Terrace** between Embassy Court and Holland Road are among the finest seafront buildings in Britain.

Walk up Waterloo Street to admire **St Andrew's Church** ❿, designed by Sir Charles Barry, architect of the House of Commons, and **The Old Market** ⓫ (tel: 01273-201 801; www.theoldmarket.com), now a performance venue. Both were built to serve the district's well-to-do residents. Continue north to Western Road then turn west to wander through Brunswick Place into **Brunswick Square** ⓬, an outstanding square with a lovely public garden.

The architects for much of Brunswick Town were Charles Busby, Amon Wilds and Amon Henry Wilds, who had designed the Kemp Town Estate a year or so earlier. Construction here in Hove progressed faster than in Kemptown and by 1828, Brunswick Square was complete, with the last section of Brunswick Terrace finished in 1840. To discover how their interiors looked when they were first built, book a tour of the lovingly restored **Regency Town House** ⓭ (13 Brunswick Square; tel: 01273-206 306; www.rth.org.uk; see website for dates).

Early Victorian Hove

Continuing west, the next open space is the serene **Adelaide Crescent** ⓮, designed in 1830 and built during the early Victorian era, and **Palmeira Square** ⓯, site of the doomed Antheum. This ambitiously large botanical conservatory was set to be the Eden Project of its era, but shoddy building work caused the whole structure to collapse just before it was due to open in 1833.

Brunswick Square.

Looking southwest from Adelaide Crescent, you'll the first of the jaunty string of **beach huts** on **Hove Esplanade** ⑯. This broad promenade, set well back from the road, has a little café and is popular with walkers and skateboarders. It overlooks a section of beach that's usually quiet and peaceful; on breezy days, you may see kitesurfers scudding past. From here, it's a wonderful walk of a little over a mile (2km) back to central Brighton, following the line of the sea.

Eating Out

Bucket and Spade Café
26–8 Kings Road Arches; tel: 01273-220 222; www.bucketandspadecafe.co.uk; Mon–Fri 9am–6pm, Sat–Sun 9am–7.30pm.
Aimed at families visiting the nearby paddling pool, this is a great place to grab a sandwich, salad or burger. The cheery name sums it up – it's a happy little seaside café where all that's missing is the sand. £

Caribou Rooms
55 Brunswick Street East; tel: 01273-723 911; www.caribourooms.com; Mon–Sat 9am–5.30pm, Sun 9.30am–5pm.
In an airy and elegant Regency building, this bohemian café serves wonderful healthy breakfasts – think homemade granola or poached eggs on sourdough toast with a vitamin smoothie – and fresh, simple lunches such as soup, sandwiches and jacket potatoes. £

The Gingerman
12A Norfolk Square; tel: 01273-326 688; www.gingermanrestaurant.com; Tue–Sun 12.30–2pm and 7–10pm.
This award-winning restaurant has done much to raise Brighton's profile as a place to eat out. In a rather small, bistro-style room that can be noisy when full – which it usually is – it serves expertly prepared and beautifully presented modern British cuisine. The assiette of desserts is a treat. £££

Iydea
106 Western Road; tel: 01273-965 904; www.iydea.co.uk; Mon–Sat 9.30am–10pm, Sun 9.30am–5.30pm.
Another award-winner, this time for vegetarian cooking, Iydea is a cool canteen-style restaurant where freshly made flans, bakes and salads are ranged behind the counter. You simply point at whatever you'd like; everything is delicious. £

The Lion and Lobster
24 Sillwood Street; tel: 01273-327 299; www.thelionandlobster.co.uk; bar open Mon–Thu 11am–1pm, Fri–Sat 11am–2am, Sun noon–midnight; bar food daily noon–10pm, restaurant Mon–Fri 5–10pm, Sat–Sun noon–10pm.
Rich in traditional character, this unpretentious city pub serves hearty fare such as venison burgers, smoked haddock with poached egg and slow roasted pork with black pudding. There's live jazz on Sunday evenings. ££

The Set
33 Regency Square; tel: 01273-855 572; www.thesetrestaurant.com; daily 12.30–3pm and 6–9.30pm.
The Set began as a pop-up before settling into Artist Residence, one of Brighton's edgier boutique hotels. Its open kitchen prepares tasting menus which use leaves, herbs and flowers grown in the chefs' own urban garden. The decor is modish, with recycled timber tables, hessian sack cushions and old classroom chairs. £££

Ditchling Beacon.

Tour 4

The Downs North of Brighton

On this 33-mile (53km) tour of Brighton's rural hinterland, you'll drive through beautiful rolling countryside and enjoy hikes to ancient fortifications with stunning views

North of Brighton and Hove, the hills and woods of the South Downs National Park rise like a wave before you. Spend a day or two exploring this swathe of green, and you'll discover peaceful footpaths leading to stunning viewpoints looking north over the Weald or south to the sea.

Nestled at the foot of the Downs are the attractive little towns of Steyning and Ditchling. Steyning was a busy river port from Saxon times until the 14th century, when the Adur began to silt up, leaving the port and its brooding defence, Bramber Castle, marooned. Later, it had another lease of life as a coaching stop, as did handsome, arty Ditchling, further east. Both now have a delightful jumble of historic houses from many eras.

Highlights

- Steyning
- St Mary's House, Bramber
- Devil's Dyke
- Ditchling
- Ditchling Beacon

CISSBURY RING

Start from the **Storrington Rise car park ❶** on Worthing's northern outskirts. To find it, turn east off the A24 (Findon Road) into May Tree Avenue, then bear left into Storrington Rise. From here, it's a 20-minute walk up to **Cissbury Ring** (www.national trust.org.uk/cissbury-ring), one of the largest Iron Age hill forts in Europe, covering 65 acres (26 hectares).

Woods Mill Nature Reserve

Around 4 miles (6km) northwest of Bramber, this pretty little woodland reserve is the headquarters of the Sussex Wildlife Trust (www.sussex wildlifetrust.org.uk). In summer, you may hear nightingales in the trees or see dragonflies hovering over the pond.

Its grassy ramparts crown a chalk promontory with wonderful views of the coast – on a clear day, you can see all the way to the Isle of Wight.

Sheep and rabbits have kept the grass short for centuries, allowing rare chalkland butterflies and wild orchids to thrive. The site also offers good birdwatching, with migrant flycatchers, redstarts and whitethroats landing here in spring and autumn.

CHANCTONBURY RING

Return to the A24 and head north past the village of **Findon**, famous for its September Sheep Fair, held since 1261. At the Washington Roundabout, turn east along the A283 for 1.6 miles (2.6km) then south into the signposted lane leading to **Chanctonbury car park ❷**.

A scenic circular hike of around 2.5 miles (4km) climbs steeply through woodlands then follows the **South Downs Way** to **Chanctonbury**

Ring, an Iron Age hill fort which can be seen for miles. When the beeches on top were planted in the mid-18th century, the stunted growth of the central trees brought about the discovery of a Roman temple. The grove was devastated by the 1987 hurricane but has been slowly regrowing.

Flint mines, burial grounds and a shepherds' dew pond are also woven into Chanctonbury's past. So, too, are demonology and witchcraft: a number of strange sightings and occurrences have been reported here.

STEYNING

Back on the A283, drive southeast to **Steyning ❸**, an appealing small town

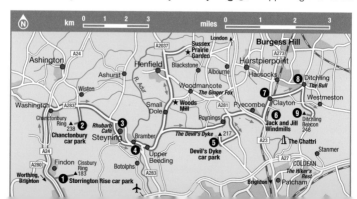

Chanctonbury Ring.

in the lee of the Downs, dotted with independent shops and Tudor, Georgian and Victorian houses. Fine old timber-framed Wealden hall houses with jettied fronts and heavy Horsham stone roofs are found on Church Street, leading off the High Street.

The **Church of St Andrew and St Cuthman** marks the site of an Anglo-Saxon church founded by Steyning's patron saint. Cuthman, an eighth-century hermit, is best known for his compassionate care for his disabled mother, who he pushed around in a wheelbarrow. His tomb became an important pilgrimage site and by the ninth century, Steyning's significance was such that the father of Alfred the Great, King Ethulwulf was buried here. His remains were later moved to Winchester Cathedral, but his tombstone remained and can be seen in the porch of the present-day church, which dates from around 1100.

The decorative grandeur of the church shows how prosperous Steyning used to be. It has the most impressive Norman nave in Sussex, with beautifully carved stone arch-

es and capitals and a heavy wooden door with sanctuary rings; the hounded could cling to these to claim refuge. The sturdy tower of chequered stone and flint is a Tudor addition.

Opposite the church, the friendly, volunteer-run **Steyning Museum** (tel: 01903-813 333; www.steyning museum.org.uk; Tue–Wed and Fri–Sat 10.30am–12.30pm, 2.30–4pm) focuses on local history.

BRAMBER

From Steyning, continue southeast to **Bramber ❹**, turning off the A283

Sussex Prairie Garden

Serene and inspiring, the Sussex Prairie Garden (tel: 01273-495 902; www.sussexprairies.co.uk; June–Oct Mon and Wed–Sun 1–5pm) is a must for plant enthusiasts. After wandering through its huge, naturalistic beds of flowers, dotted with contemporary sculptures, you can drink in the view over tea and homemade cake on the terrace.

Clayton Hill

Standing proudly on Clayton Hill, just east of the A273, are Jack and Jill, a landmark pair of 19th-century windmills. As you'd expect, this is a wonderfully breezy place with far-reaching views of the tranquil, folded South Downs. Jill (www.jill windmill.org.uk; May–Sept Sun 2–5pm) has been restored to full working order by volunteers and grinds local wheat into flour, which is often available to buy on the spot.

roundabout to **Bramber Castle** (www.english-heritage.org.uk). There's not much left of this Norman motte and bailey castle – it's more of a grassy picnic spot than a heritage site – but the tower-like remains of its gatehouse suggest its former power. Commissioned in the 1070s by William de Braose, a follower of William the Conqueror, it guarded the River Adur.

De Braose's **Church of St Nicholas**, south of the castle, has survived far better. Though much altered over the centuries, it contains some rare 11th-century stone carvings and

is considered the oldest Norman church in Sussex.

Further east along Bramber's pretty village street is one of Britain's finest 15th-century timber-framed buildings, **St Mary's House** (tel: 01903-816 205; www.stmarysbram ber.co.uk; May–Sept Thu and Sun 2–6pm). It was once a monastic inn; before the river retreated, ships would moor outside. Saved from demolition in the 1940s, the interiors and gardens have been lovingly restored and enhanced by the present owners. Look out for the Painted Room and the ancient gingko tree.

DEVIL'S DYKE

From Bramber, continue east along the A2037 (Henfield Road). After Upper Beeding, it bears north; you may wish to stay on this road to visit the **Woods Mill Nature Reserve** (see page 48), the pleasant village of **Henfield** and the **Sussex Prairie Garden** (see page 49).

Alternatively, one mile (1.6km) beyond the outskirts of Upper Beeding, turn east off the A2037 to enjoy a scenic drive along Edburton Road and Poynings Road. This country lane hugs the foot of the Downs, pass-

Mist hanging in the Devil's Dyke.

Jill Windmill on Clayton Hill.

ing three hamlets of pretty cottages: **Edburton**, **Fulking** and **Poynings**. Both Edburton and Poynings have ancient flint-walled churches, while near The Shepherd and Dog pub in Fulking there's a bubbling natural spring. South Downs shepherds used to drive their flocks down here to wash them before shearing.

After Poynings, turn south to climb up Saddlescombe Road. After Saddlescombe Farm, where there's a café, turn right along Devil's Dyke Road and right again after the golf club. The road soars through open countryside to **Devil's Dyke car park ❺**, which perches above **Devil's Dyke**, Britain's deepest dry valley, carved out during the Ice Age. The hilltop (711ft/217 metres) has an Iron Age hillfort, a pub and superb panoramic views of the Weald.

Victorian tourists used to love this beauty spot, climbing up from Poynings via a steep-grade railway to enjoy amusements at the top. Today, you may see kites, hang gliders and paragliders riding the breeze.

CLAYTON

Return to Saddlescombe Road and drive north. At the roundabout, turn east onto the A281 to Pyecombe, then join the A23 to Brighton, turning off at the A273 to Hassocks. Keep following the signposts for Hassocks, turning north to climb Clayton Hill, where you might want to divert east along Mill Lane to visit the **Jack and Jill Windmills ❻** (see box). Back on the A273, turn east into Underhill Road to visit the simple but very special Anglo-Saxon **Church of St John the Baptist** in the village of **Clayton ❼**. Inside, you'll find superb frescoes depicting the Last Judgement, painted by monks from St Pancras Priory in Lewes in the 11th or 12th century.

The Chattri

High on the Downs above Brighton, this poignant domed memorial marks the site of the funeral pyre of 32 injured Hindu and Sikh soldiers who were cared for in Brighton during World War I, but could not be saved. Thousands of Indian servicemen were hospitalised in the Royal Pavilion, where nine separate kitchens catered for their preferences.

Ditchling Museum of Art and Craft.

DITCHLING

North of Clayton, follow New Road (B2112) to **Ditchling** ❽, a well-groomed downland village with artistic associations and a High Street lined with picturesque historic buildings.

Wings Place, found 100yds/metres west of the main crossroads on West Street, is one of England's finest Tudor private homes. This motley jumble of timber and brick was, like Anne of Cleves House in Lewes,

View across wheatfields towards Ditchling Beacon.

one of the properties awarded to Anne of Cleves by Henry VIII as part of her divorce settlement. It stands opposite the 12th-century **St Margaret's Church**, whose east window was designed in 1947 by leading Ditchling artist Charles Knight. The churchyard contains carvings by local craftsmen.

In the early 20th century, Ditchling was a focal point of the Arts and Crafts movement, and it remains a creative enclave today. Its past and present residents include sculptor and typographer Eric Gill, his teacher Edward Johnston, who designed the London Transport font, the popular children's book illustrator Raymond Briggs and master goldsmith Anton Pruden. A collection of work by Ditchling artists can be seen at the beautifully designed **Ditchling Museum of Art and Craft** on Lodge Hill Lane, northwest of the church (tel: 01273-844 744; www.ditchling museumartcraft.org.uk;   Tue–Sat 11am–5pm; Sun noon–5pm), which has an enticing café and shop.

DITCHLING BEACON

The road south of Ditchling leads steeply up to **Ditchling Beacon** ❾, an early Iron Age hillfort site with superb views of the Weald. At 814ft (248 metres), this is one of the highest points in the South Downs and for London to Brighton cyclists, making it to the top is a triumph. This is a favourite starting point for South Downs walks and, in summer, a good place to see chalkhill blue butterflies and round-headed rampion, known as the Pride of Sussex, a wildflower with a head of up-curled blue petals.

Eating Out

Steyning
Rhubarb Café
27 High Street; tel: 01903-814 317; daily 9.30am–5.30pm.
This cute little café serves good coffee and excellent light lunches – salads, quiches, wraps and the like. Standard teatime treats include gluten-free apple and almond cake and home-made fruit cordial. There's an appealing courtyard garden at the back. £

Albourne and Saddlescombe
The Ginger Fox
Muddleswood Road, Albourne; tel: 01273-857 888; www.thegingerfox. com; bar open daily 11.30am–midnight; food served Mon–Fri noon–2pm and 6–10pm, Sat noon–3pm and 6.30–10pm, Sun noon–4pm and 6–9pm.
Only 7 miles (11km) from Brighton but surrounded by lush green countryside, this pub is a little oasis. It looks and feels like a large family house that's been converted into a hostelry, with a kids' play area, newspapers and big comfy chairs enhancing the homeliness. The menu features excellent British fare, with hearty roasts on Sundays. £££

The Hiker's Rest
Saddlescombe Farm, Saddlescombe Road; tel: 01273-857 712; Mar–Nov Wed–Fri 11am–4pm, Sat–Sun 11am–5pm.
Offering a warm welcome to walkers, cyclists and motorists alike, this farmyard pitstop, right on the South Downs Way, offers tasty home-made treats, including sandwiches, soup and the owner's trademark cakes. £

Devil's Dyke
The Devil's Dyke
Dyke Road, Poynings; tel: 01273-857 256; www.vintageinn.co.uk; Mon–Fri noon–11pm, Sat 10am–11pm, Sun noon–10.30pm.
This reliable country pub has a fabulous location on the crest of the Downs. As well as real ale and almost 40 wines, it offers standard pub fare such as pies and steaks, with great value set menus. The No. 77 bus from Brighton Pier and Brighton Station to Devil's Dyke turns around here, so it's hugely popular. £

Ditchling
The Bull
High Street; tel: 01273-843 147; www.thebullditchling.com; bar open Mon–Fri 11am–11pm, Sat 8.30am–11pm, Sun 8.30am–10.30pm; food served Mon–Fri noon–2.30pm and 6–9.30pm, Sat noon–9.30pm, Sun noon–9pm.
Highly acclaimed for its excellent food, The Bull is a gastropub with rooms which prides itself on sourcing local, seasonal ingredients from trusted suppliers. With low ceilings and open fires, it's particularly cosy on grey days. Brightonians love to nip out of town to eat here at weekends, so it can get very busy. £££

Tour 5

Lewes

Explore the quirky, arty downland town of Lewes, historic capital of Sussex, on this 2.5-mile (4km) walking route around its centre

Spilling down from its Norman castle to the banks of the River Ouse, the county town of Lewes is modestly proportioned, character-ful and a pleasant place to hunt for crafts and antiques. One of only three towns lying wholly within the South Downs National Park (along with Midhurst and Petersfield), it has steep streets with fine views of roll-ing hillsides and chalky cliffs.

Strategically sited to guard the gap in the Downs cut by the Ouse, Lewes was an important Saxon set-tlement, with two mints. When the Normans arrived, they built not only the impressive castle but also a huge priory with a church the size of Westminster Abbey, fragments of which can still be seen.

Highlights

- Lewes Castle
- Lewes High Street
- Cliffe
- Southover Grange Gardens
- Anne of Cleves House

LEWES CASTLE

Start your stroll at **Lewes Castle** ❶ (Castle Gate; tel: 01273-486 290; www.sussexpast.co.uk; Mar–Oct Tue–Sat 10am–5.30pm, Sun–Mon 11am–5.30pm; Nov–Feb Tue–Sat 10am–3.45pm, Sun–Mon 11am–3.45pm, closed Mon in Jan), the high point of the town. Within a year of the Battle of Hastings, William the Conqueror's forces built timber defences on this

Lewes Castle Gate – the castle is unusual in having two mottes.

Views of Lewes Castle

You can see Lewes Castle from miles away, but it's oddly invisible from much of the town centre. While the views from Castle Gate are impressive, there's a more romantic, distant view from The Paddock and Baxter's Field, a grassy urban park reached via Paddock Road or Bradford Road.

commanding site, later replacing them with a sturdy stone fortress.

Romantically ruined, the castle has been a tourist attraction since the mid-1800s and occasionally hosts open-air plays and concerts.

Climb the 14th-century barbican and the 11th-century keep, and you can enjoy views south to the Ouse estuary at Newhaven and across to Firle Beacon in the east. To the northwest is Harry Hill, from which in 1264 Simon de Montfort and his supporters launched the attack that began the Battle of Lewes. De Montfort soundly defeated Henry III, forcing him to sign the Mise of Lewes which brought parliamentary government to England. Inside the barbican is a small lo-

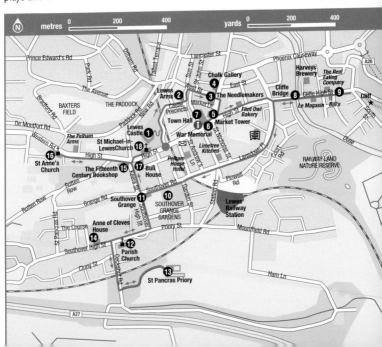

cal history museum featuring plans of the castle, a model of Lewes as it was in the 1880s and a crossbow demo.

LEWES ARMS AND THE NEEDLEMAKERS

The neat, walled lawn on the north-east side of the castle was once a tilting yard, but has been a bowling green since at least 1640, making it Britain's oldest. From here, follow the Castle Precincts downhill to the curved frontage of the **Lewes Arms ❷**, one of around 1,250 listed buildings in and around Lewes. This pub, a favourite meeting place for local societies, is known for its quirky customs and competitions.

From the pub, walk north along Mount Place then turn right into West Street. The old candle and needle factory building by the car park is **The Needlemakers ❸** (tel: 020-7700 4114; www.needlemakers.co.uk; Mon–Sat 9am–5.30pm, Sun 11am–4.30pm), an attractive emporium of craft, gift and vintage shops with a good café.

From the east end of West Street, divert a few steps along North Street to visit the **Chalk Gallery ❹** (tel: 01273-474 477; www.chalkgallery lewes.co.uk; Tue–Sun 10am–5pm), one of the best places in this supremely arty town to buy work by local painters, ceramicists and jewellers. Next, head south along Market Street. On Friday mornings, a produce market is held in the red brick **Market Tower ❺**, built in 1792.

Pells Pool

The much-loved Pells Pool (Brook Street; www.pellspool.org.uk; mid-May to mid-Sept; see website for opening times) opened on the north side of town in 1861 and is the oldest freshwater lido in Britain. Fed by a natural spring, it's not heated, so in cooler weather you may want to act like a triathlete and kit up in a wetsuit and hat. On warm days, it's the perfect place to be, with a main swimming pool, a paddling pool and a grassy garden for picnics. The main pool's generous proportions (46 x 23 metres) make it popular with fitness fanatics as well as the splashabout crowd. Birds sing from the trees as you swim, and ducks quack from the brook nearby.

View over Lewes from the castle.

Turn back to walk northeast past the War Memorial and down High Street. On the way you'll pass **Albion Street**, edged with a Regency terrace which could have been transplanted from Brighton.

CLIFFE

At the bottom of High Street, cross into the precinct leading east towards the River Ouse. It's dotted with stalls selling fruit, cheese and charcuterie on the first and third Saturday mornings of the month, when the Lewes Farmers' Market takes place.

Hogging the view from **Cliffe Bridge 8**, built in 1732, is the Victorian Gothic tower of **Harveys Brewery** (www.harveys.org.uk), sometimes wryly referred to as Lewes Cathedral. John Harvey's company, the oldest independent brewery in Sussex, has been operating since the late 1700s. It's possible to tour the premises, but there's usually a two-year waiting list.

Legendary Bonfire Night celebrations in Lewes.

LEWES TOWN HALL

At the **War Memorial 6** marking the junction of Market Street and High Street, bear southwest. The red brick **Town Hall 7**, 20yds/metres from the memorial, stands on the site of the 14th-century, Catholic-owned Star Inn, in front of which 17 Protestants were burned at the stake for their faith between 1555 and 1557. Before their execution, the last ten were imprisoned beneath the inn in cellars which still exist, lit by a grill in the pavement.

These gruesome deaths are commemorated in anti-Catholic rituals re-enacted throughout Sussex each autumn. A granite memorial to the martyrs, overlooking the town on Cliffe Hill, was unveiled in 1901.

Towards the end of the 18th century, the Star Inn was demolished and the Town Hall constructed. A century later, the building was remodelled, gaining a fine Jacobean staircase rescued from Slaugham Place near Haywards Heath.

Bonfire Night

To say Lewes celebrates Bonfire Night with a bang is putting it mildly. On 5 November, it all kicks off – the town is closed to traffic and huge crowds gather to watch the Bonfire Society parades and firework displays. The Bonfire Boys, as they're known, carry flaming crosses and drag barrels of burning tar through the narrow streets to commemorate Lewes' 17 Protestant martyrs. Each society proceeds to its own bonfire site where satirical effigies are set alight amid volleys of rockets. While most of the effigies are topical, there's always one of the pontiff at the time of the Gunpowder Plot, Pope Paul V, which gets torched to lusty yells of 'Burn the Pope!'

Harveys Brewery.

Continue over the bridge to **Cliffe High Street** ❾, a pleasantly old-fashioned street lined with cafés, boutiques and shops selling antiques and vintage oddments. Harveys Brewery has a shop here and there's even a harpsichord workshop in the area.

SOUTHOVER

Retrace your steps across Cliffe Bridge and the precinct, then walk half a mile southwest, turning south along Friars Walk then west along Lansdowne Place and Southover Road. At the junction with Garden Street is the entrance to **Southover Grange Gardens** ❿, a public park with colourful beds of flowers.

Southover Grange ⓫ itself is a 16th-century mansion built of limestone filched from the ruins of the nearby priory. In its north wing is the **Sussex Guild Shop and Gallery** (tel: 01273-479 565; www.thesussex guild.co.uk; daily 9am–5pm), representing highly talented local craftworkers.

Turn south along Southover High Street and bear west at the mini roundabout. After **Southover Parish Church** ⓬, which has a chapel dedicated to the priory's founders,

turn south into Cockshut Road and follow the lane under the railway line. The shattered remains of **St Pancras Priory** ⓭ (www.lewespriory.org.uk) are in the park beyond. Construction of the priory by the Benedictine Order of Cluny began in 1082. It grew into one of the wealthiest monasteries in England.

Back on Southover High Street, turn west to visit **Anne of Cleves House** ⓮ (tel: 01273-474 610; www.sussex past.co.uk; Mar–Oct Tue–Sat 10am–5pm, Sun–Mon 11am–5pm; Nov–Dec and Feb Tue–Sat 10am–4pm, Sun–Mon 11am–4pm). This late medieval timber-framed hall house was one of

Antique Shops in Lewes

In Lewes, there's seemingly a shop selling antiques and bric-a-brac around every corner. While Cliffe is the hub, other spots worth checking out are Lewes Flea Market at 14A Market Street and Church Hill Antiques Centre at 6 Station Street, both converted churches. Much of the furniture for sale in Lewes is modest in scale, to suit the town's bijou properties.

the properties given to Anne of Cleves as part of her annulment settlement from Henry VIII in 1541, although she never lived here. It's now a museum, with rooms dressed in Tudor style, a collection of Wealden iron fire backs and a garden inspired by 16th-century planting schemes, complete with a medlar tree.

THE HIGH STREET

Head back to Southover Grange then continue uphill via **Keere Street**, a steep, cobbled lane lined with pretty cottages. It leads north to the High Street, emerging at **The Fifteenth Century Bookshop ⑮**, a wonderfully rickety-looking timber-framed building.

At this point you could divert west to **St Anne's Church ⑯**, the oldest church in Lewes, much of which dates back to the 12th century. From here back to the Town Hall, the High Street is tightly packed with facades from different eras, brick or flint, galleried, tile-hung or mathematical-tiled, many with Georgian windows.

Bull House ⑰, east of Keere Street at 92 High Street, is the 15th-century home of the Sussex Archaeological Society. The 18th-century po-

litical activist Thomas Paine lived here from 1768 to 1774; Two years later, his writings inspired the rebels of the American Revolution to declare independence from Britain. Around 20yds/metres east, on the north side of the High Street, is **St Michael-in-Lewes Church ⑱**, notable for its 13th-century round tower, slender spire and neatly knapped flint walls. Only two other Sussex churches, at Southease and Piddinghoe, have round towers.

The High Street, Lewes.

Eating Out

Bill's

56 Cliffe High Street; tel: 01273-476 918; www.bills-website.co.uk; Mon–Fri 8am–10.30pm, Sat 8am–11pm, Sun 9am–10.30pm.

Ever since local lad Bill Collison first opened a café offering imaginative, market-fresh dishes in his greengrocers shop, Lewes residents have flocked in. Bill's is now a chain and this, the place where it all started, has lost some of its homespun charm, but it remains supremely family-friendly; you'll have to fight for a table at busy times. ££

Flint Owl Bakery

209 High Street; tel: 01273-472 769; www.flintowlbakery.com; Mon–Sat 9am–5pm.

This cool, contemporary bakery has stacks of crisp organic loaves in the window and heaps of pastries on the counter, all baked in nearby Glynde using local sea salt and spring water. You can enjoy a salad or a speciality coffee at the farmhouse table inside or in the charming walled courtyard at the back. £

Limetree Kitchen

14 Station Street; tel: 01273-478 636; www.limetreekitchen.co.uk; Wed–Sat noon–2.30pm and 6.30–9.30pm, Sun noon–2.30pm.

In a pleasantly shabby-chic space that's airy by day and cosy by night, Limetree Kitchen uses local ingredients to produce short, seasonal modern European menus. The chef, a trained chocolatier, makes sure every dish looks a treat – a dab of sauce here, a sprinkle of leaves and petals there. ££

Le Magasin

50A Cliffe High Street; tel: 01273-474 720; Tue–Thu noon–11pm, Fri–Sat noon–midnight, Thu–Sat 8am–10pm, Sun 9am–5pm.

This European-style café is one of the best places in Lewes for a healthy cooked breakfast or an indulgent croissant, just as it should be – crispy on the outside, soft on the inside. It also serves excellent lunches and, on Thursday, Friday and Saturday evenings, sharing platters and tapas. ££

The Pelham Arms

High Street; tel: 01273-476 149; www.thepelhamarms.co.uk; Tue–Thu noon–11pm, Fri–Sat noon–midnight, Sun noon–10.30pm.

The Pelham Arms is the perfect English country pub, in the heart of Lewes – think low beams, open fires and real ale. The bar and kitchen champion local producers such as Ridgeview Wine in Burgess Hill, Flint Owl Bakery in Glynde and Brighton's Infinity Foods. The Sunday roasts are legendary and even the bar snacks are a cut above. ££

Pelham House Hotel

St Andrew's Lane; tel: 01273-488 600; www.pelhamhouse.com; daily 11am–9pm.

The largest garden in the centre of town belongs to this elegant hotel, a favourite for posh wedding parties and weekends away. Non-residents can enjoy breakfast in the lounge bar, afternoon tea on the terrace or anything from a light lunch to an elaborate dinner in the restaurant. £££

The Real Eating Company

18 Cliffe High Street; tel: 01273-402 650; www.real-eating.co.uk; Mon–Sat 8.30am–9pm, Sun 10am–9pm.

Popular with young families, this bistro-style restaurant prides itself on making more or less everything on the menu from scratch, often using ingredients fresh from the countryside and coast around Lewes. There's a traditional roast lunch with huge Yorkshire puddings every Sunday. ££

Tour 6

Ouse Valley, Cuckmere Valley and the Sussex Heritage Coast

This 44-mile (70km) driving tour, with optional walks, takes in magnificent chalk cliffs, medieval villages and the downland landscapes adored by the Bloomsbury Group

The sweep of coastal downland between Lewes and Eastbourne is one of the very loveliest parts of the South Downs National Park. Easily accessible from Brighton, the hills, dells and cliffs around the River Ouse and the winding Cuckmere attract paragliders, horse riders and dog walkers, while music lovers converge at Glyndebourne for world-class opera in a sumptuous setting.

Start with an afternoon in Bloomsbury-in-Sussex, the rural refuge of Virginia Woolf, Duncan Grant, Vanessa Bell and their bohemian entourage of writers, artists, and intellectuals. After that, there's wonderful countryside to explore, dotted with

Highlights

- Charleston Farmhouse
- The Long Man of Wilmington
- Alfriston
- Cuckmere Haven
- Birling Gap
- Beachy Head

pretty villages, flint-walled churches and welcoming country pubs with low beams, gleaming beer taps and crackling fires.

MONK'S HOUSE

Begin your tour in **Rodmell**, 11 miles (18km) east of central Bright-

View from Firle Beacon towards the South Downs.

on. A weatherboarded cottage near the north end of the village, **Monk's House** ❶ (tel: 01273-474 760; www.nationaltrust.org.uk; Apr–Oct Wed–Sun 1–5pm), was the country retreat of writer Virginia Woolf and her husband Leonard from 1919. They were Sussex regulars, having spent a few years hopping between London and a rented house in Bed-

Self portrait by Vanessa Bell at Charleston Farmhouse.

dingham or visiting Virginia's sister Vanessa Bell in Firle.

In 1940, after their flat in Bloomsbury was bombed, the Woolfs made Rodmell their permanent home but, tragically, Virginia drowned herself in the nearby River Ouse the following year. The cottage remains as it was while they were in residence, with modest furniture and piles of books. In the pretty garden outside is Virginia's writing shed, where she worked on many of her novels.

GLYNDE

Drive north via Kingston to the A27, then east past the Bronze Age hill fort of **Mount Caburn** to **Glynde Place** ❷ (tel: 01273-858 224; www.glynde.co.uk; May–June Wed–Thu and Sun 1–5pm). Rather plain apart from its clocktower and wyvern-topped gates, this Elizabethan manor is still a family home, lined with ancestral portraits. In summer, festivals and events take place in its spacious parkland with views of the Weald.

Next to the house is a rare Palladian church, **St Mary the Virgin**, built in 1765 for former resident Richard Trevor, bishop of Durham. John Ellman

the Gage family, one of whom introduced greengages to Britain from France. They've lived here since the 15th century, rebuilding their Tudor manor in the present Georgian style in the mid-18th century, using stone from the ruins of St Pancras Priory in Lewes. Among their treasures are Sèvres porcelain, French furniture and paintings by Van Dyck, Gainsborough and Reynolds.

Firle is a quiet but atmospheric downland village with a convivial pub, **The Ram Inn**, and **St Peter's**, a 13th-century church with a 1980s stained-glass window by John Piper, who also designed Chichester Cathedral's richly coloured altar tapestry. This was the parish church of the Sussex-based Bloomsbury set; the churchyard contains the graves of the artists Duncan Grant and Vanessa Bell and Vanessa's son Quentin.

Bloomsbury-in-Sussex

Back on the A27, you'll pass **Middle Farm** (www.middlefarm.com) on your way east to **Charleston Farmhouse** ❹ (www.charleston. org.uk; Apr–Oct Wed–Sat 1–6pm, Sun 1–5.30pm), which Grant and Bell rented from 1916. They decorated the interior with fluid, painterly mu-

of Glynde Farm, the original breeder of Southdown sheep, is buried here, as is Audrey Mildmay, the opera singer who in 1934, with her husband John Christie, created the celebrated opera house at **Glyndebourne** (tel: 01273-812 321; www.glyndebourne. com), a mile (1.6km) to the north.

FIRLE, CHARLESTON AND BERWICK

Return to the A27 and continue east to **Firle Place** ❸ (tel: 01273-858 307; www.firle.com; June–Sept Sun–Thu 2–4.30pm) at the foot of **Firle Beacon**. It's the ancestral home of

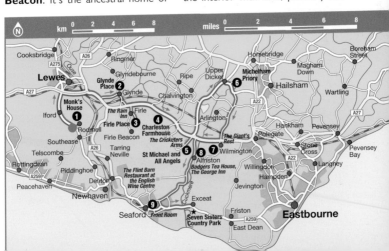

rals and hosted sparkling house parties at which Virginia Woolf, Dora Carrington, Lytton Strachey, Roger Fry and John Maynard Keynes were regular guests. The house, studio and garden have been beautifully preserved in tribute to their distinctive aesthetic and way of life.

Further work by the Bloomsbury artists can be seen 3 miles (5km) away at **St Michael and All Angels** ❺ (Berwick; tel: 01323-896 008; www.berwickchurch.org.uk; daily 10am–dusk), a 12th-century church that was much modified in the 1850s. In 1941, Bishop Bell of Chichester, a champion of ecclesiastical tradition and 20th-century art, commissioned Grant and Bell to decorate the interior with large wall paintings inspired by pre-Reformation frescoes. The pair enlisted a motley assortment of family, friends and locals as models. Part Biblical, part war memorial, the results were strikingly avant garde.

Drusillas Park

Everything about Drusillas (Alfriston Road, Berwick; tel: 01323-874 100; www.drusillas.co.uk; Apr–Oct daily 10am–6pm, Nov–Mar daily 10am–5pm), a multi-award-winning zoo and adventure park, is family-friendly, from the animals (mostly small and cute, with lemurs, monkeys and meerkats making star appearances) and the Hello Kitty and Thomas the Tank Engine attractions to the well-chosen restaurant menu. There are also fun play areas and educational activities.

MICHELHAM PRIORY

Drive north past Berwick Station to Upper Dicker, then turn east to **Michelham Priory** ❻ (tel: 01323-844 224; www.sussexpast.co.uk; daily Mar–Oct 10.30am–5pm, Nov–Dec and Feb 11am–4pm) which was founded by Augustinian canons in

Michelham Priory.

View towards the Long Man of Wilmington.

1229. The east and north wings date from this time; the west wing was added when the building was converted into a Tudor hunting lodge and farm. Attractively set on an island on the River Cuckmere, it's surrounded by water meadows, a working watermill and the longest water-filled moat in England. The gardens are full of interest, with medieval plantings inspired by the Book of Hours.

WILMINGTON

Turn southeast along Michelham Priory Road, then follow the signposts to **Wilmington** ❼ along Caneheath, Bayleys Lane and Thornwell Road, crossing the A27 to enter the village. **St Mary and St Peter's Church** was once part of the 11th-century Benedictine priory which stood nearby; the wizened yew tree in the churchyard, supported by heavy posts, is thought to be at least 1,000 years old.

Carved into the flank of Wendover Hill, south of the village, is the **Long Man of Wilmington**, Britain's tallest chalk figure. Skilfully drawn so that the proportions look correct from afar, its origins are mysterious; it was perhaps created by locals who had seen the Cerne Abbas giant on their travels and wanted to create something similar. During World War II, it was painted green to prevent enemy aviators using it as a landmark.

ALFRISTON

To reach the gorgeous downland village of **Alfriston** ❽, follow the narrow lanes south and west via Lullington, or head west along the A27 to the roundabout then turn south along Alfriston Road, passing the **English Wine Centre** and **Drusillas Park**.

Snuggled between rolling hills beside the River Cuckmere, Alfriston stands on the South Downs Way. Its centre, jammed with attractive medieval buildings, gallery shops and tea rooms, floods with walkers, cyclists, horse riders and other visitors in summer, but instead of feeling touristy there's a real sense of community here, thanks partly to its lively calendar of festivals and events.

Three excellent 14th-century pubs share the narrow high street. **The Star** used to be owned by Battle Abbey; extravagantly built of massive timbers and Horsham slabs, it was a top end hostelry for medieval pilgrims visiting Winchester, Chichester or Canterbury. **The George**, opposite, is a creaky and characterful old coaching inn, while **Ye Olde Smugglers Inne** was a notorious hangout in the 1700s, when contraband was big business in this part of Sussex.

On the **Tye**, Alfriston's perfect village green, is the unusually large, flint-walled **St Andrew's Church** and a beautifully preserved Wealden hall house, **Alfriston Clergy House** (tel: 01323-871 961; www.nationaltrust. org.uk; Mar–Oct Sat–Wed 10.30am–5pm, Nov–Dec Sat–Wed 11am–4pm), the first property the National Trust acquired. It's plastered with lime and tallow and floored with rammed chalk sealed with soured milk. Also on the Tye is the tasting room for **Rathfinny** (www.rathfinnyestate.com), the vineyard south of the village.

SEAFORD

Four miles (6.5km) southwest of Alfriston via **High and Over**, a hilltop with glorious views of the Cuckmere meanders, **Seaford** 9 is an unassuming, old-fashioned coastal town, and that's its charm. Its quiet railway terminus, high street and long, pebbly shore feel worlds apart from busy, noisy Brighton: apart from a great little beach hut selling drinks and slices of home-made cake, there's little to distract you from the serious business of swimming or simply chilling out.

At the eastern end of the esplanade, a Napoleonic era Martello Tower has been converted into a local history museum (tel: 01323-898 222; www.seafordmuseum.co.uk; Apr–Oct Wed and Sat 2–4pm, Sun 11am–4pm; Nov–Mar Sun 11am–4pm). Like Doctor Who's Tardis, it's much bigger on the inside than it looks.

SUSSEX HERITAGE COAST

Follow the A259 east out of Seaford to swoop between open pastures to **Cuckmere Haven**, where footpaths lead past salt marshes, water meadows and the lazy, bird-rich River Cuckmere to the sea. Look up the

The George Inn in Alfriston dates back to the 15th century.

South Downs Way

The southeastern limits of this magnificent National Trail (www.nationaltrail.co.uk/south-downs-way) undulate through classic downland landscapes with regular glimpses of steely-grey or chalky-blue sea. At the walker-friendly village of Alfriston, the path splits. While the main bridleway heads east via Jevington or west over Firle Beacon, those on foot can opt to stride south to Cuckmere Haven and along the Sussex Heritage Coast to Eastbourne, one of the best stretches of all.

The majestic Seven Sisters.

valley towards Alfriston and you'll often see paragliders soaring over the **High and Over chalk horse**, a Victorian folly created by the landowner and his farmworkers as a prank.

There are several options for lovely walks, bike rides or river trips in this area, particularly from **Exceat ⑩** on the east bank. **Friston Forest**, to the north, has glades of beeches and evergreens, while the **Seven Sisters Country Park** to the south preserves rare chalk grassland, home to round-headed rampion, scented wild thyme and adonis blue butterflies. Bikes and canoes are available to hire.

Seven Sisters to Beachy Head

The **Seven Sisters**, a string of springy-turfed hills ending in chalk cliffs, are icons of the **Sussex Heritage Coast**. The undulating South Downs Way follows them east to **Birling Gap ⑪**, where waves crash against the shore, nibbling it away and causing a terrace of houses to shrink over the years; a National Trust visitor centre (tel: 01323-423 197; www.nationaltrust.org.uk; daily 10am–4pm) explains the process.

There's another coastal landmark further east – the magnificent **Beachy Head ⑫**, topped by **Belle Tout Lighthouse**. Built to last in the 1830s, the lighthouse was a costly mistake; it was often shrouded in mist and was perilously close to the rapidly eroding cliff edge. In 1902, the more practical Beachy Head Lighthouse was built at the foot of the cliff, and in 1999 Belle Tout was shifted inland to prevent it tumbling into sea. It's now a bed and breakfast.

In the village of **East Dean ⑬**, inland from Birling Gap, you can learn about traditional farming at the **Seven Sisters Sheep Centre** (tel: 01323-423 207; www.sheepcentre. co.uk; lambing season Mar–Apr daily 10.30am–5pm, shearing season July–Aug daily 10.30am–5pm) or relax on the delightful green before catching a bus back to Exceat.

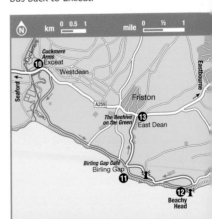

Eating Out

Firle

The Ram Inn

The Street, Firle; tel: 01273-858 222; www.raminn.co.uk; food served Mon–Sat noon–3pm and 6.30–9.30pm, Sun noon–4pm and 6.30–9.30pm.

This pub with rooms takes local food sourcing so seriously that the seasonal menu may feature wild mushrooms gathered on the Downs, meat from a neighbouring farm and mackerel caught by the village vicar. A pretty garden offers plenty of space for kids to run about. ££

Berwick

The Cricketers Arms

The Village; tel: 01323-870 469; www.cricketersberwick.co.uk; Mon–Fri 11am–10.30pm, Sat 11am–11pm, Sun noon–10.30pm.

Appealingly village pub in an English country cottage with a flower-filled garden, just down the road from St Michael and All Angels, known as the Bloomsbury Group church. Well-kept real ale and tasty food, including desserts big enough to share. ££

The Flint Barn Restaurant at the English Wine Centre

Alfriston Road; tel: 01323-870 164; www.englishwinecentre.co.uk; Tue–Thu noon–3pm, Fri–Sat noon–3pm and 6.30–9.30pm, Sun noon–3pm.

This smart but understated eatery serves excellent, good value lunches and delicious dinners featuring local ingredients. The owners offer a huge range of wines by the glass and are glad to make recommendations to match each course. ££

Wilmington

The Giant's Rest

The Street; tel: 01323-870 207; www.giantsrest.co.uk; food served Mon–Sat noon–2pm and 6–9pm, Sun noon–9pm.

In an Edwardian house with a homely atmosphere, this gastropub has an impressive menu featuring delicious pub classics, French-inspired dishes such as chicken liver pâté or steak with creamy mushroom sauce and an excellent African-style peanut and vegetable stew. ££

Alfriston

Badgers Tea House

13 North Street; tel: 01323-871 336; www.badgersteahouse.com; Mon–Fri 9.30am–4pm, Sat–Sun 10am–4.30pm.

Alfriston is heaven on earth for tea-and-scone lovers and Badgers works hard to stay ahead of the field, with scrumptious sandwiches and cakes, excellent service and a delightful courtyard garden. £

The George Inn

High Street; tel: 01323-870 319; www.thegeorge-alfriston.com; food served Mon–Sat noon–2pm and 6–9pm, Sun noon–9pm.

This 15th-century inn oozes historic character, with crackling fires, wooden pews and low beams strung with dried hops, bunting and fairy lights. Good Sussex beer, restaurant-style fare and a clutch of upstairs bedrooms make it a popular choice with locals and visitors alike. ££

Seaford

Front Room

42 High Street; tel: 01323-895 383; www.frontroomseaford.co.uk; Sun–Thu 9am–5pm, Fri–Sat 9am–5pm and 7.30–11.30pm.

Tucked behind Seaford's sleepy shopping streets, this funky little café would be perfectly at home in Brighton, with its sunny courtyard, jauntily mismatched furniture and hand-knitted tea cosies. It serves top notch coffee, tasty breakfasts and leafy salads. £

Eastbourne Pier.

Tour 7

Eastbourne and 1066 Country

This two-mile (3km) stroll around Eastbourne and 32-mile (30km) drive to Battle reveals some of the many historic sites between the Sussex Heritage Coast and the High Weald

Eastbourne seafront is the legacy of Victorian landowner and developer William Cavendish, the seventh Duke of Devonshire, who envisioned it as a holiday resort 'built by gentlemen, for gentlemen'. Even today, Eastbourne's conservative atmosphere is worlds apart from youthful, energetic Brighton. Culturally, however, it's catching up, as are Bexhill and Hastings. All three have award-winning contemporary art centres with real creative clout.

There's a real sense of history on this coast, which has defended Britain for almost 1,000 years. The last successful invasion was in 1066, when the Normans landed at Pevensey and defeated the Anglo-Saxons at what is now Battle.

Unlike their counterparts at Beachy Head or indeed Dover, the brown

Highlights

- Towner Gallery, Eastbourne
- Eastbourne seafront
- Pevensey Castle
- Herstmonceux Castle
- De La Warr Pavilion, Bexhill
- Hastings Old Town
- Jerwood Gallery, Hastings

cliffs of Hastings have never featured in a propaganda poster or wartime song, but they're a quintessentially English coastal rampart, nonetheless. Twice attacked by the French in the Hundred Years War, Hastings hosted a 12,000-strong garrison during the Napoleonic Wars. Among those who served here was Arthur Wellesley, who later earned the title Duke of Wellington.

EASTBOURNE

Begin your tour with a stroll around **Eastbourne**, a stalwart of the British seaside, with old-fashioned floral displays, brass bands and hotels lit by twinkling chandeliers.

While much of the central shopping area between the **station ❶** and the pier is unremarkable, there are independent shops and pubs to be found by walking south down Grove Road then east along South Street in **Little Chelsea ❷**. Next, turn south to visit **How We Lived Then ❸** (20 Cornfield Terrace; tel: 01323-737 143; www.how-we-lived-then.co.uk; daily from 10am), a one-of-a-kind museum of shopping crammed with vintage merchandise, from World War II rations to wedding dresses.

Continue south along Chiswick Place to the foot of Devonshire Park.

> ## Hop on the Bus
>
> Brighton & Hove (www.buses.co.uk) bus 12/12X makes travelling to Eastbourne a breeze. Superbly scenic, the route hugs the coast most of the way, with great views of Cuckmere Haven and the Downs above Beachy Head from the top deck. Once you're in town, Stagecoach (www.stagecoachbus.com) or City Sightseeing (www.citysightseeing.com; Mar–Oct) buses can whizz you around and Stagecoach route 99 will take you on to Pevensey, Bexhill and Hastings.

The intimate and ornate **Devonshire Park Theatre ❹** (tel: 01323-412 000; www.eastbournetheatres.co.uk) is one of the gems of Victorian Eastbourne and the **Devonshire Park Lawn Tennis Club** (tel: 07581-076 730; www.devonshireparkltc.co.uk) hosts

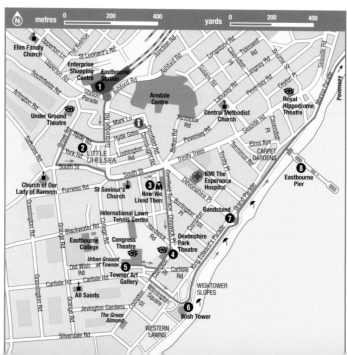

Contemporary art on display at Towner Art Gallery.

world class championships each year. You can dose up on local history at the **Eastbourne Heritage Centre** (2 Carlisle Road; tel: 01323-411 189; www.eastbourneheritagecentre.co.uk).

On the south side of Devonshire Park, the refreshingly modern **Towner Art Gallery ⑤** (tel: 01323-434 670; www.townereastbourne.org.uk; Tue–Sun 10am–5pm) has been shaking up the south coast art scene since 2009, when the renowned Towner Collection moved here from its former home in Eastbourne Old Town. Thought-provoking exhibitions of new photography, painting and multimedia art complement its 20th-century works, including an important body of paintings by Sussex artist Eric Ravilious.

The seafront

South of Devonshire Park is the **Wish Tower ⑥** (www.wishtower.org.uk), one of the 74 numbered Martello towers built between Folkestone and Seaford in the Napoleonic era. Unusually, this one is practically unaltered, and volunteers sometimes open it to the public.

In the 1850s, Eastbourne blossomed into one of the best planned Victorian resorts on the south coast. The Duke of Devonshire insisted that there should be no beachfront shops to mar the elegance of the **seafront**, which had spacious carriageways, ornamental flowerbeds, lawns and a large **bandstand ⑦** beside the pebble beach. These remain in use today, as does the privately owned, Grade I listed **Eastbourne Pier ⑧**, designed by Eugenius Birch in the 1870s. Tragically, however, part of it caught fire in 2014 and may never be fully restored.

From the pier, you could continue another half mile along the seafront to the **Redoubt Fortress** (tel: 01323-410 300; www.eastbournemuseums.co.uk; Mar–Nov Tue–Sun 10am–5pm), which is similar in age to the Wish Tower and contains an excellent military museum.

PEVENSEY

From Eastbourne seafront, drive northwest past Sovereign Harbour to **Pevensey Bay**, then turn inland to **Pevensey** and follow the signpost off the A259 to the splendidly time-worn ruin of **Pevensey Castle ⑨** (Castle Road; tel: 01323-762 604; www.english-heritage.org.uk; daily 10am–5pm).

It's layered in history, its hefty outer wall built in the fourth century to defend a Roman fort against Saxon pirates. At the time, Pevensey was an island at the mouth of the River Ashburn. When William the Conqueror's army invaded in 1066, it was here that they landed, later building a timber fortress on the site, followed by a massive stone keep and bailey walls, much of which can still be seen today. In World War II, Pevensey was prepared for action once again, with pillbox-style horizontal slits built into the masonry.

Nearby, amid a string of historic cottages on the High Street, is **St Mary's Church, Westham**, founded in the late 1000s and considered the oldest Norman church in England. The 15th-century stained glass in its east window is exceptionally rare: in Oliver Cromwell's time, iconoclastic parliamentarians smashed similar examples elsewhere in Sussex. **St Nicolas Church**, east of the castle, is around a century younger than St Mary's; the crosses in the porch walls were carved by returning crusaders.

Head east out of Pevensey, turning north at Pevensey Roundabout along Wartling Street to pass the serene open marshlands of the **Pevensey Levels National Nature Reserve**.

HERSTMONCEUX CASTLE

After Wartling, turn west to **Herstmonceux Castle ⑩** (tel: 01323-833 816; www.herstmonceux-castle.com; Apr–Oct daily 10am–6pm), a majestic fortified manor rising from a glassy moat.

Herstmonceux has always been a residence rather than a fortress. It was designed to resemble a French chateau and in the 15th century was England's first large-scale brick building, making it extremely fashionable. Now part of Queen's University in Kingston, Ontario, its gardens, which are open to the public, are themed; one is full of plants mentioned in Shakespeare's plays.

From 1947 to 1989, the castle and its grounds belonged to the Royal Greenwich Observatory. Its telescopes occupied a collection of buildings with brick walls and green copper domes, designed to blend into the Sussex countryside, but before long growing light pollution from Eastbourne forced the astronomers to move. Their labs are now the Observatory Science Centre (tel: 01323-832 731; www.the-observatory.org; Feb–Nov daily, Dec–Jan Sat–Sun), with excellent interactive exhibits and historic telescopes.

Herstmonceux Castle.

Medieval Rye

Well worth a detour, this charming little town was a bustling medieval port. Now separated from the sea by a swathe of protected marshland four miles wide, its castle, Ypres Tower, is a museum (tel: 01797-226 728; www.rye museum.co.uk) and its pretty streets are home to independent shops and galleries. Don't miss Mermaid Street, a cobbled lane lined with medieval cottages, or Camber Sands, a bike ride away, one of the best beaches in Sussex.

The De La Warr Pavilion, an arts centre in Bexhill-on-Sea.

DE LA WARR PAVILION

Return to Wartling and head for the A259, either by returning to Pevensey Roundabout or by taking the short-cut via Horsewalk, the narrow country lane beside Wartling's Lamb Inn. Continue east to **Bexhill-on-Sea**, where the **De La Warr Pavilion** ⓫ (tel: 01424-229 111; www.dlwp.com; daily Apr–Oct 10am–6pm, Nov–Mar 10am–5pm) dominates a tidy and appealing stretch of seafront.

This centre for contemporary arts occupies an iconic 1930s building named after Herbrand Sackville, ninth Earl De La Warr, the young socialist mayor who commissioned it. His specification was ahead of its time, requiring it to be simple, light and attractive, with a welded steel frame and large windows. Modernist architects Erich Mendelsohn and Serge Chermayeff delivered this and more, adding sleek staircases and cutting-edge light fittings. Restored in the early 2000s, the centre hosts exhibitions, talks, films and live performances.

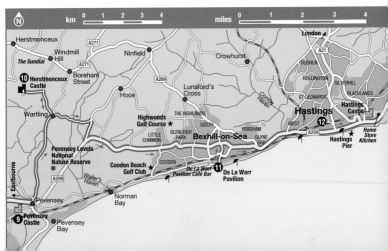

HASTINGS

Back on the A259, drive east over the cliffs to **Hastings** ⓬. Presiding over **St Leonards**, the up-and-coming west side of town, is Marine Court, a Modernist building shaped like a cruise ship. St Leonards also has fine Regency terraces designed by James and Decimus Burton and pleasant green spaces on the seafront and on Maze Hill. **Warrior Square**, the showiest square, is edged with grand Victorian mansion flats.

Hastings' oldest quarters lie east of the pier. This salty seadog of a town was one of the 12th-century Cinque Ports, charged with keeping the royal fleet supplied with ships; the tax breaks and laxity it enjoyed in return made it a smugglers' haven. **Hastings Museum and Art Gallery** (off Bohemia Road; tel: 01424-451 052; www.hmag.org.uk; Apr–Oct Tue–Sat 10am–5pm, Sun noon–5pm, Nov–Mar Tue–Sat 10am–4pm, Sun noon–4pm) focuses on this and other aspects of local history.

Hastings Old Town

The **Old Town** in the Bourne Valley, east of Hastings Castle, is a characterful, bohemian jumble of lanes, with dozens of cafés and independent shops on George Street and High Street and lichen-roofed, timber-framed homes on All Saints Street.

Adding a fizz of modernity to this historic quarter is the **Jerwood Gallery** (Rock-a-Nore Road; tel: 01424-728 377; www.jerwoodgallery.org; Tue–Sun 11am–5pm), its facade clad in hand-glazed mathematical tiles in a striking pewter-black shade. It shows paintings from its 20th- and 21st-century British art collection, which features works by Stanley Spencer, LS Lowry and Walter Sickert.

On the beach beyond, called the Stade, are Hastings' famous net shops, shop being the old term for workplace.

Fishing boat in Hastings's historic fishing quarter.

Fishermen used to hang their nets and ropes in these tall, skinny timber sheds, a tradition dating back to the 19th century when land was so valuable they could only afford tiny plots. Their walls, once heavily tarred, are now painted black instead.

BATTLE ABBEY

Leave Hastings by continuing along the A259, then turn northwest to follow the B2093 and A2100 to **Battle Abbey** (tel: 01424-775 705; www.english-heritage.org.uk; Apr–Sept daily 10am–6pm; Oct daily 10am–4pm, Nov–Mar Sat–Sun 10am–4pm). Founded by William the Conqueror in penance for the lives lost at the Battle of Hastings, the high altar of this Benedictine monastery stood at the spot where King Harold fell on 14 October 1066. It was destroyed after the Dissolution and the grandest remaining fragment is the gatehouse, fortified during the Hundred Years War. A modern exhibition centre and audio guides provide context, and volunteers re-enact the bloodcurdling events of 1066 every year.

Eating Out

Eastbourne

Farm

15 Friday Street; tel: 01323-766 049; www.farmfridaystreet.com; Mon–Fri 10am–11.30pm, Sat 9am–11.30pm, Sun 9am–11pm; food served Mon–Fri noon–9.30pm, Sat 9am–9.30pm, Sun 9am–9pm.

In a 17th-century farmhouse that's now surrounded by residential streets in the Friday Street area of town, this large pub restaurant serves standards such as sandwiches, cod and chips, gammon with piccalilli and Sunday roasts. Log fires and candles add to the atmosphere. ££

The Green Almond

12 Grand Hotel Buildings, Compton Street; tel: 01323-734 470; www.the greenalmond.com; Tue–Thu 10am–4pm, Fri–Sat noon–4pm and 7–10pm; buffet lunch served Tue–Sat noon–3pm.

This family-run vegetarian bistro is in a smart parade of shops behind the Grand Hotel. It offers a reasonably priced buffet lunch, with salads, dips and seed mixes so tempting you'll be piling your plate as high as you can. Fixed price suppers available on Fridays and Saturdays. £

Urban Ground at Towner

Devonshire Park, College Road; tel: 01323-434 670; www.towner eastbourne.org.uk; Tue–Sun 10am–4.30pm.

After lapping up some Ravilious or the latest contemporary installation at the Towner Art Gallery, head upstairs to relax over a drink and a croissant or flatbread at this modern café with lovely South Downs views. There's also a branch in the town centre at 2A Bolton Road, open Mon–Sat 7.30am–6pm and Sun 9am–5pm. £

Herstmonceux

The Sundial

Gardner Street; tel: 01323-832 217; www.sundialrestaurant.co.uk; Tue–Sat noon–2pm and 7–9.30pm, Sun noon–3.30pm.

The Sundial is a much-praised French fine dining restaurant serving dishes such as seabass with saffron and basil or lamb noisette with ratatouille and polenta. Vegetarians and vegans are advised to discuss their preferences in advance as the standard menu concentrates on meat and fish. £££

Bexhill-on-Sea

De La Warr Pavilion Café Bar

Bexhill Marina; tel: 01424-229 119; www.dlwp.com; daily 10am–5.30pm; cooked breakfast served Sat–Sun 10–11.30am, lunch served Mon–Fri noon–2.30pm, Sat–Sun noon–3pm.

With big, sea-facing windows flooding the space with light, even on overcast days, this modern eatery is an airy and enjoyable place to enjoy a lunch of soup or Sussex lamb chops or, at weekends, a breakfast of homemade granola with yogurt and honey followed by classic eggs Benedict. ££

Hastings

Home Store Kitchen

36 High Street; tel: 01424-447 171; www.homestore-hastings.co.uk; Sat–Sun noon–4.30pm.

Alastair Hendy of AG Hendy & Co Home Store has created something unique – a beautiful vintage hardware shop in a painstakingly restored Tudor house. At the back is a room where those with the foresight to book a table can tuck into a weekend lunch of local shrimps, crab or lobster, prepared by Hendy himself.

Bodiam Castle.

Tour 8

The High Weald

Enjoy splendid gardens, historic houses and a moated castle on this 54-mile (87km) drive through the High Weald Area of Outstanding National Beauty

With scattered copses, sandstone outcrops and sunken lanes, the landscapes of the High Weald are quite different from the South Downs. Extending beyond Sussex into Surrey and Kent, this was once the most wooded part of England and many beautiful, ancient forests survive, their glades carpeted with bluebells in spring. As early as the 14th century, prosperous Londoners made the region their country retreat, bringing wealth to its farms and villages.

To enjoy this appealing corner of rural England to the full, you could spend a couple of days or more exploring, staying at The Griffin Inn in Fletching or one of the country B&Bs along the way.

Highlights

- Nymans
- Wakehurst Place
- Sheffield Park
- Bluebell Railway
- Bodiam Castle
- Great Dixter

NYMANS

Conveniently close to the A23, around 17 miles (28km) from Brighton, this romantic garden makes a good starting point. **Nymans ❶** (Handcross; tel: 01444-405 250; www.nationaltrust.org.uk/nymans; garden daily Mar–Oct 10am–5pm, Nov–Feb 10am–4pm; house daily Mar–Oct 10am–4pm) was succes-

The ruined manor at Nymans, unchanged since the 1940s.

sively the home of German-born stockbroker Ludwig Messel, his son Leonard and granddaughter Anne Messel (Lady Rosse, mother of Lord Snowdon).

Ludwig Messel's topiary-edged garden rooms, their borders bursting with colour, were inspired by the Arts and Crafts movement. Leonard added a large mock-Gothic manor and magnolias, rhododendrons and camellias grown from seeds sourced in the Himalayas and the Andes. After the manor was gutted by fire in the 1940s, only part of it was rebuilt, leaving the rest a picturesque ruin.

WAKEHURST PLACE

From Nymans, follow the B2110 north-east to Turners Hill and the B2028 south to **Wakehurst Place ❷** (near Ardingly; tel: 01444-894 066; www.nationaltrust.org.uk/wakehurst-place; Mar–Oct daily 10am–6pm, Nov–Feb daily 10am–4.30pm, free guided tours May–Dec daily 11.30am). The grounds of this Elizabethan mansion are managed by the Royal Botanic Gardens, Kew. Extensive and diverse, they contain beautiful horticultural specimens of national and global importance.

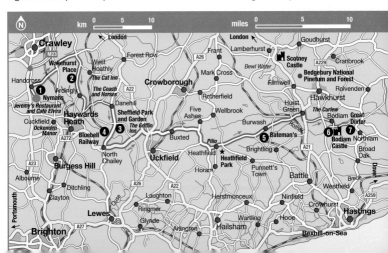

Sheffield Park and Garden.

A barrel-vaulted exhibition, research and cold-storage facility near the modern visitor centre houses Kew's Millennium Seed Bank. Its goal is to conserve 25 percent of the world's plant species by 2020, as a safeguard against extinction. Outside, an array of raised beds represent threatened British habitats including shingle beach and chalk downland.

The estate has formal gardens, a nature reserve and magical woodlands containing the National Plant Collections of birch and southern beech trees. There are also some spectacular conifers, including a giant redwood near the house that's festooned with lights each winter, making it the tallest living Christmas tree in Britain.

SHEFFIELD PARK AND GARDEN

Follow the B2028 south through Ardingly, turning east along Stonecross Lane and Keysford Lane via Horsted Keynes to Danehill, then south along the A275 to **Sheffield Park and Garden** ❸ (near Uckfield; tel: 01825-790 231; www.nationaltrust. org.uk/sheffield-park-and-garden;

daily 10am–5pm). Originally designed by Capability Brown, this impressive country estate has splashes of interest in every season, with superb daffodils, bluebells, azaleas and rhododendrons, dazzling autumn colours in the maple, birch and hickory trees and mellow mists over the lakes in winter. Sheffield Park House is closed to the public but adds Gothic drama to the landscape.

BLUEBELL RAILWAY

Half a mile (0.6km) further down the A275 is the Sheffield Park terminus of the **Bluebell Railway** ❹ (tel: 01825-720 800; www.bluebell-railway.com; Apr–Sept daily, Oct–Mar limited service). This much-loved heritage railway has been run by volunteers since 1960; the first season attracted 50,000 passengers. From Sheffield Park, where there's a museum and locomotive shed to visit, steam trains chuff their way to Horsted Keynes, Kingscote and East Grinstead, arriving back a little under two hours later. The stations, decked out with vintage adverts, clocks and luggage, are part of the charm.

BATEMAN'S

Around 22 miles east via the A272 and A265 is **Bateman's** ❺ (Burwash; tel: 01435-882 302; www.nationaltrust.org.uk/batemans; house daily 11am–5pm, garden daily 10am–5.30pm) the Jacobean house where Rudyard Kipling and his American wife Caroline lived between 1902 and the late 1930s.

The Kiplings loved Bateman's for its historic character and tranquil setting – a welcome change from their previous home, Rottingdean (see page 38), which was becoming a busy tourist destination. The interior remains as it was in the 1930s, with shelves crammed with books and Rudyard's desk overflowing with papers. Rugs, art and artefacts reflect the author's deep connection to India, where he spent his early childhood, late teens and early twenties.

BODIAM CASTLE

Continue east along the A265 and south along the A21, then follow the signpost east to **Bodiam Castle** ❻ (near Robertsbridge; tel: 01580-830 196; www.nationaltrust.org.uk/bodiam-castle; daily 10am–5pm). This graceful castle, built in the late 14th century for Sir Edward Dalyngrigge, a well-connected knight, is one of the loveliest landmarks in Sussex. On still days, reflects its fairytale turrets are mirrored in its huge, peaceful moat. To add to the romance, it has never seen hostilities, apart from some minor incidents during the Civil War.

While the stone exterior appears immaculate, the interior is a ruin with plenty to fire the imagination, from spiral staircases to battlements and murder holes. Cheerful volunteers in historic dress are often on hand offer demonstrations of 14th-century customs and organise activities for kids.

GREAT DIXTER

Head south from Bodiam then east via Ewhurst Green to Northiam, turning northwest along Dixter Road to **Great Dixter** ❼ (tel: 01797-252 878; www.greatdixter.co.uk; Apr–Oct Tue–Sun garden 11am–5pm, house 2–5pm). The house is a fascinating jumble of 15th- and 16th-century buildings, beautifully combined and remodelled in the style of a medieval manor by Edwin Lutyens in the 1910s. But it's the garden that most visitors come to see. For garden writer and experimental plantsman Christopher Lloyd, who was born at Great Dixter and lived here for most of his life, Arts and Crafts style gardening was a passion.

Yew-hedged garden rooms, each with a different mood from the next, provide a prelude to the magnificent Long Border. There's also a tranquil wildflower meadow, swaying with grasses in summer.

A vintage steam trains puffs along the Bluebell Railway.

Eating Out

West Hoathly
The Cat Inn
North Lane; tel: 01342-810 369; www.catinn.co.uk; food served Mon–Thu noon–2pm and 6–9pm, Fri–Sat noon–2.30pm and 6–9.30pm, Sun noon–2.30pm.

Part 16th-century, part Victorian with modern touches, this is a fine Sussex gastropub. There's real ale on tap and excellent pub grub such as steak, mushroom and ale pie, or slow braised pork belly with black pudding. ££

Near Haywards Heath
The Coach and Horses
Coach and Horses Lane, Danehill; tel: 01825-740 369; www.coachand horses.co; food served Mon–Thu noon–2pm and 6.30–9pm, Fri noon–2pm and 6.30–9.30pm, Sat noon–2.30pm and 6.30–9.30pm, Sun noon–3pm.

An attractive country pub with a panelled bar, low beams and a grassy beer garden. The emphasis is firmly on quality local food and drink, with several Sussex ales and wines on offer and an ever-changing menu featuring delicious ingredients, from Fletching asparagus to freshly caught hake. £££

Jeremy's Restaurant and Café Elvira
Borde Hill Lane, Borde Hill; tel: 01444-441 102; www.jeremysrestaurant. co.uk; Tue–Sat 12.30–2.30pm and 7–10pm, Sun 12.30–2.30pm.

With an elegant dining room and a pretty terrace, this award-winning restaurant is a favourite for country weddings and upmarket celebrations. The seasonal menu offers beautiful and original flavour combinations, such as South Downs lamb with chive gnocchi, hazelnuts and turnips. £££

Ockenden Manor
Ockenden Lane, Cuckfield; tel: 01444-416 111; www.hshotels.co.uk; daily noon–2pm and 7–9.30pm.

Head chef Stephen Crane has won a Michelin star several years in a row at this fine restaurant in a rambling Sussex manor house. He creates beautifully executed dishes using local ingredients. With attentive staff, twinkling chandeliers and scenic views, this is one for special occasions.

Fletching
The Griffin Inn
High Street; tel: 01825-722 890; www.thegriffininn.co.uk; food served Mon–Fri noon–2.30pm and 7–9.30pm, Sat noon–3pm and 7–9.30pm, Sun noon–3pm and 7–9pm. Like all the best country pubs, The Griffin is snug in winter and glorious in summer, with a cosy interior and a large, family-friendly garden overlooking miles of rolling countryside. The kitchen produces first class British fare. ££

Heathfield
Pilio
53 High Street; tel: 01435-863 376; www.piliobistro.co.uk; Tue–Sat 10am–4pm and 6.30–10pm.

Run but a couple from Thessaly, this intimate little bistro offers authentic Greek dishes such as feta-stuffed peppers and keftedakia meatballs. There's good Italian coffee, Greek beer and, of course, plenty of retsina. £

Bodiam
The Curlew
Junction Road; tel: 01580-863 376; www.thecurlewrestaurant.co.uk; Tue–Sat noon–2.30pm and 6.30–9.30pm, Sun noon–2.30pm and 6.30–9pm. This former coaching inn offers top notch modern British cooking. Head chef Michael Mealey conjures up imaginative combinations in every dish. The prices may be steep but, for such a high standard, it's good value. £££

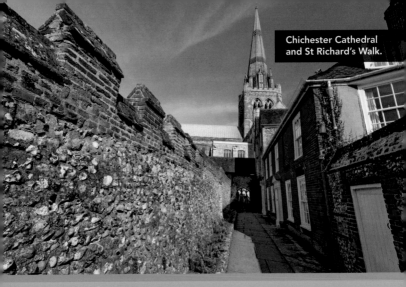

Tour 9

Chichester

Discover traces of the past on a 2-mile (3km) walk around the cathedral city of Chichester, shaped by the Romans, Saxons, Normans and Georgians

Soaring over a low-lying coastal plain at the foot of the Downs, the spire of Chichester's Norman cathedral has drawn pilgrims to southwest Sussex for centuries. When the Normans arrived in the 11th century, this was already an ancient settlement, strategically sited on the River Lavant, close to a large, safe harbour. Celtic tribesmen were living in the area when the Romans invaded in 43 AD and founded the city of Noviomagus Reginorum.

Four centuries later, it was renamed after Cissa, one of Sussex's Saxon conquerors; by the ninth century, it was among the largest of Alfred the Great's fortified settlements. Today Chichester is an attractive city with the feel of a market town. Its his-

Highlights

- Chichester Cathedral
- Bishop's Palace Gardens
- The Novium Museum
- Pallant House Gallery
- Chichester Festival Theatre

toric centre is graced by fine Georgian buildings, many of which are listed.

CHICHESTER MARKET CROSS

Compact and with a straightforward, pedestrian-friendly layout, Chichester's city centre is easy to explore on foot. The natural place to start is the early 16th-century **Market Cross** ❶ which marks the centre of the

Chichester High Street and the distinctive Market Cross monument.

city's compass. It stands at the crossroads of the four main streets, North, South, East and West, which were laid out by the Romans. Each street leads to a gate in the old city walls.

Octagonal, with stone buttresses, panels, rosettes and arches, the market cross is like a medieval cathedral in miniature. The clock, the bust of Charles the Martyr and the lantern on top are relatively recent additions to the structure. Commissioned in 1500 by the benefactor Bishop Storey, the cross sheltered poor traders from the elements until the early 1800s, when the Market Hall (now a smart little shopping arcade called the **Butter Market**) was built nearby on North Street to a design by John Nash.

CHICESTER CATHEDRAL

Standing right in the heart of the city, immediately southwest of the Market Cross on West Street, **Chichester Cathedral** ❷ (tel: 01243-782 595; www.chichestercathedral.org.uk; daily 7.15am–6pm in winter, 7.15am–7pm in summer; voluntary donation) is the greatest church building in Sussex. Gothic and Romanesque in style, it was founded by the Normans in 1076 on the site of an important Roman

building, possibly a basilica; a fragment of floor mosaic, discovered during maintenance work in 1966, has been preserved in situ in the quire.

Notable for its free-standing bell tower and double aisles, unique among medieval cathedrals in Britain, the building is a true survivor, having weathered several fires and, in the 19th century, the total collapse of the spire. Maintenance is a constant concern and to keep the fabric intact, the cathedral supports a local team of traditional craftsmen, particularly stonemasons, but also joiners and metalworkers. Their skills are in demand all over the country.

Cathedral Peregrines

Members of the RSPB have been keeping an eye on the two successive pairs of peregrine falcons which have nested in the turrets of Chichester Cathedral since 2001. At the time of writing, they have successfully reared over 50 chicks. Between March and June, you can watch live nestcam footage of their comings and goings on a screen in the Cloisters Café.

An Inspiring Landmark

Said to be the only cathedral spire in Britain that can be seen from the sea, Chichester's 276ft (84-metre) -high landmark keeps popping back into view as you wander the city centre and the surrounding suburbs and meadows. In town, there are striking views from the upper windows of the Novium and serene views from the Bishop's Palace Gardens, Priory Park and the Chichester Canal.

Altars and sacred art

Entrance to the cathedral is through the west portico. The interior is a light, graceful space, adorned with medieval sculptures and modern art. As you look down the nave you're immediately struck by a blaze of colour behind the high altar: this is an abstract tapestry depicting the Holy Trinity, designed by John Piper in 1966.

The most celebrated 20th-century artwork in the building is a vibrant, ruby-red stained glass window by Marc Chagall in the retrochoir, behind the high altar. Inspired by the words 'Let everything that has breath praise the Lord' (Psalm 150), it was created in 1978 when Chagall was 90 years of age, and was his last commissioned work.

Also in the retrochoir is an altar commemorating St Richard of Chichester, a 13th-century bishop. A relic of the saint is buried beneath it. Behind the altar is a large tapestry, woven in the 1980s by a local and German craftworkers, and there's a statue

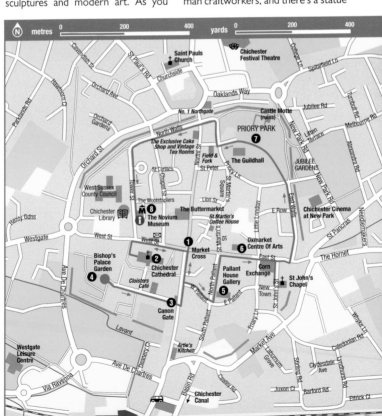

Chichester Festival Theatre

When the Chichester Festival Theatre (Oaklands Park; tel: 01243-781 312; www.cft.org.uk) opened in 1962, its first artistic director was Sir Laurence Olivier, who assembled a company which included Sybil Thorndike, Michael Redgrave and Joan Plowright. With Britain's first thrust stage and rough concrete walls in Brutalist style, the building was strikingly modern in the 1960s. A recent makeover has improved the sightlines and spruced up the lobbies, giving this highly respected theatre a new lease of life.

of St Richard to one side. The original shrine, a medieval pilgrimage site, was destroyed under Henry VIII in 1538.

Nearby, in the Chapel of St Mary, is a 1961 painting by Graham Sutherland. Called *Noli Me Tangere* (Do not hold me), it shows Christ on a staircase to heaven, appearing to Mary Magdalene, who assumes he's the gardener.

The Cathedral Close

Head back to the Market Cross, turn south along South Street and then west through the 16th-century **Canon Gate** ❸ into Canon Lane. This area, tucked under the cathedral's skirts, is the **Cathedral Close**, a city-centre hamlet of beautiful houses built for resident and visiting clergy. They include the pretty 15th-century terraced cottages of Vicar's Close and the Grade I listed Bishop's Palace, founded in the 14th century.

While the palace remains a private residence, a large part of its grounds, **Bishop's Palace Garden** ❹, at the end of Canon Lane, is a public park. This lovely spot is an oasis of well-tended lawns, flower beds and trees, partly edged by the city walls. Founded by the Romans, Chichester's walls have been modified over the centuries but remain remarkably intact. The section in the gardens includes a Roman bastion.

PALLANT HOUSE GALLERY

Walk back along Canon Lane and through Canon Gate, then turn left along South Street and right along West Pallant to the Gulbenkian Prize winning **Pallant House Gallery** ❺ (tel: 01243-774 557; www.pallant. org.uk; Tue–Wed 10am–5pm, Thu 10am–8pm, Fri–Sat 10am–5pm, Sun

The Holy Trinity Tapestry designed by John Piper.

View of the cathedral from Bishop's Palace Garden.

11am–5pm; free except for special exhibitions) on North Pallant. It contains one of the world's most significant collections of modern British art.

In a district of beautiful Georgian streets, Pallant House is an elegant Queen Anne townhouse, built in 1712 for a wealthy wine merchant. A modern extension with an eco-friendly geothermal heating system was added in 2006. The gallery displays an impressive, rotating art collection by mainly 20th-century British painters, including Graham Sutherland, Paul Nash, Ivon Hitchens and Henry Moore. Many were amassed by Walter Hussey, Dean of Chichester Cathedral from 1955–77, who, with Bishop Bell, was instrumental in giving modern British art a place in the cathedral. There are regular exhibitions of other works, including winning entries in the annual National Open Art Competition.

EAST STREET, LITTLE LONDON AND PRIORY PARK

Head north along North Pallant to East Street, Chichester's main shopping street, where herds of livestock were once driven to market. On St Andrew's Court, in the quarter north of East Street known as **Little London**, a deconsecrated 13th-century church is now home to the **Oxmarket Centre Of Arts ⑥** (tel: 01243-779 103; www.oxmarket.com; Tue–Sun 10am–4.30pm; free), which holds exhibitions by emerging local artists.

Back on East Street and heading east, you'll pass a neoclassical building on the corner of Baffins Lane, fronted by Doric style columns. This was the **Corn Exchange**, built in 1832. It has been used as a music hall and cinema and now houses shops and offices. Further east, **St John's Chapel** (tel: 01243-788 631; www.

Chichester Canal

Just 4.5 miles (7.2km) long and with only two locks, the Chichester Canal was originally intended as part of a long-distance waterway running all the way from London to Portsmouth. In recent years, a stretch has been restored and can be explored by rowing boat, canoe, or canal boat trip with the Chichester Ship Canal Trust (tel: 01243-771 363; www.chichestercanal.org.uk), starting from the wharf 200yds/metres south of the railway station.

Planetarium

To gaze up at the heavens, head for the South Downs Planetarium and Science Centre (Kingsham Road; tel: 01243-774 400; www.south downs.org.uk), which was opened in 2002 by former Chichester district resident, the astronomer Sir Patrick Moore. Its regular astronomy presentations are open to the general public. It's also possible to visit at other times, by appointment.

stjohnschapelchichester.co.uk) on St John's Street is a beautiful little Georgian building that has been barely changed since its construction in 1813. It occasionally hosts concerts and lectures.

Priory Park and The Guildhall

Return to East Street then turn north into East Walls and follow the rampart-like path along the old city wall. It leads to **Priory Park** ❼, a green with a cricket pitch and, beyond it, Chichester's **motte**, a grassy mound which is the last remnant of the city's

Norman castle, destroyed in the early 13th century.

Also in the park is **The Guildhall**, a 13th-century church building which was originally the chancel of a Franciscan friary. It has had several other uses since, and is now hired for weddings.

THE NOVIUM MUSEUM

From Priory Park, follow Priory Lane north and bear west to North Walls, then take the footpath alongside the city wall as far as the steps leading down to Tower Street. As you approach the cathedral, you'll pass the drum-shaped **Library and Information Centre** and reach **The Novium Museum** ❽ (tel: 01243-775 888; www.thenovium.org; Apr–Oct Mon–Sat 10am–5pm, Sun 10am–4pm, Nov–Mar Mon–Sat 10am–5pm; free). This crisp, modern building doubles as Chichester's tourist information centre and local history museum. It stands on the site of a Roman bath house, remains of which are on display. In the exhibition areas, multimedia displays and artefacts cover many aspects of Chichester's history, particularly the Roman era.

The Guildhall in Priory Park.

Eating Out

Artie's Kitchen

33 Southgate; tel: 01243-790 365;
www.artieskitchen.com; Tue–Sat
8.30am–10.30pm, Sun 9.30am–4pm.
Calling itself an artisan café, Artie's
has bags of modern attitude. The
decor is urban-rustic, with chunky
wood and steel furniture, exposed
brick walls and a counter edged
with distressed tiles. Whether you
choose banana bread or a full fry up,
breakfast is a feast, lunch options
include soup, mezze and flans and
there's a short, well-chosen evening
menu. £

Cloisters Café

Chichester Cathedral; tel: 01243-
813 590; www.chichestercathedral.
org.uk; Mon–Sat 9am–5pm, Sun
10am–4pm.
There's always a buzz in this canteen-
style café, especially in spring,
when the RSPB rig up TV screens
to monitor the movements of the
peregrine falcons which nest in the
cathedral turrets. There are indoor
and outdoor tables where you can
tuck into hot lunches, snacks and
drinks. The Sunday roast is excellent
value. All profits support the upkeep
of the cathedral. £

The Exclusive Cake Shop and Vintage Tea Rooms

47 North Street; tel: 01243-774 127;
www.exclusive-cupcakes.com; Mon–
Sat 9am–5pm.
Brimming with charm, this is a café
which makes tea time a special
occasion, with chintzy decor, lace
tablecloths, vintage china and cute
finger sandwiches. Ridiculously
tempting cupcakes, loaded with
squidgy icing, are the house
speciality. The simple lunch menu is
also a treat. There's another branch in
Midhurst. £

Field & Fork

4 Guildhall Street; tel: 01243-789
915; www.fieldandfork.co.uk; Tue–Sat
11.30am–9.30pm.
Formerly based in the Pallant House
Gallery, where they wowed the
critics, the Michelin-trained team
behind Field & Fork have moved a
few streets north to this attractive
restaurant with an airy conservatory.
The food is as good as ever, full of
vivid flavours. Everything, from the
bread to the fresh pasta and ice
cream, is made on the premises. £££

No. 1 Northgate

1 Northgate House, North
Street; tel: 01243-774 204;
www.no1northgate.co.uk; Mon–Fri
10am–midnight, Sat 9am–midnight,
Sun 9am–10.30pm.
In a converted bank near Priory
Park and the Chichester Festival
Theatre, this smartly presented bistro
and bar has white tablecloths and
sleek modern touches. The food is
contemporary and international in
style, with an antipasto platter, Thai
green curry and grilled rib eye steak
among the dishes on offer. The set
menu aimed at theatre-goers is
particularly good value. ££

St Martin's Coffee House

3 St Martin's Street; tel: 01243-786
715; www.organiccoffeehouse.co.uk;
Tue–Sat 10am–6pm.
This unique café wears its principles
on its sleeve. All the cakes are made
without butter, sugar or cream and
are proudly labelled organic and
additive-free. The building is listed,
with cosy nooks, open fires and a
jumble of vintage furniture. The
mildly eccentric owner can sometimes
be found playing sonatas on the
piano and customers are invited to
do the same. £

Art and Literature

The rich heritage, soft textures and bright sunshine of urban and rural Sussex have provided endless inspiration, from 19th-century landscape painters to 21st-century poets

Thanks partly to the effervescent influence of George, the Prince Regent, writers and painters flocked to Sussex in the 19th century. John Keats visited Chichester, Constable, Dickens and Thackeray were often in Brighton and, under the patronage of the Earl of Egremont, J. M. W. Turner spent many days at his easel at Petworth House.

Bombay-born Rudyard Kipling moved to East Sussex in 1897, at the dawn of an era in which many other creatives and thinkers sought inspiration in its peaceful coastal countryside. In his poem *Sussex*, written in 1902, Kipling expressed his deep love for the 'blunt, bow-headed, whale-backed Downs' with their sea fogs, dew ponds and 'close-bit thyme that smells like dawn in Paradise'.

The turn of the 19th and 20th centuries brought a blossoming of the Arts and Crafts movement, with decorative artists, silversmiths and designers converging on Ditchling and plantsmen creating magnificent gardens at Nymans and Great Dixter in the High Weald.

The countryside around Lewes became a hub of creativity during World War I, when conscientious objectors gravitated here. Artists Duncan Grant and Vanessa Bell, leading lights of the Bloomsbury Group, entertained many luminaries at Charleston Farmhouse,

Beachy Head by Eric Ravilious; Frank Newbould poster; Virginia Woolf.

Art Trails and Events

26 Letters Children's literature. *May* www.brightonfestival.org

Artists' Open Houses Huge network of art trails in and around Brighton. *May and December* www.aoh.org.uk

Charleston Festival Literature and talks. *May* www.charleston.org.uk

Sussex Poetry Festival Readings and events. *June* www.sussexpofest. wordpress.com

Chichester Open Studios Art trail. *July* www.chichesterarttrail.org

Eastbourne Festival Includes artists' open houses. *July* www.eastbourne festival.co.uk

Arundel Festival Includes poetry and prose. *August* www.arundel festival.co.uk

Brighton Art Fair Contemporary art sale. *September* www.brightonart fair.co.uk

Lewes Artwave Art trail in and around town. *September* www.art wavefestival.org

Small Wonder Short stories. *September* www.charleston.org.uk

Made Brighton Contemporary craft fair. *November* www.brighton-made.co.uk

the country retreat that they shared. Vanessa's sister Virginia Woolf loved Sussex, too, spending many years in nearby Rodmell, until her depressions, exacerbated by the war and the battles in the skies overhead, drove her to suicide in the Ouse in 1941.

The Sussex watercolourist Eric Ravilious grew up in Eastbourne and returned to Sussex as a young man in the 1930s to sketch and paint its Saxon villages and Downland landscapes. Created at a time of uncertainty, with war on the horizon, his works evoke a fragile nostalgia laced with foreboding.

In contrast, the images of Sussex created in the 1940s by the graphic artist Frank Newbould are confident and brave. One depicts the summer funfair on Alfriston Tye, another a South Downs shepherd tending his flock on the hills near East Dean. These tender English scenes became War Office propaganda posters, captioned *Your Britain: fight for it now.*

With notable collections at Chichester Cathedral and the Pallant House, Cass Foundation, and Towner and Jerwood galleries, modern art in Sussex is currently on a high.

Boats in Bosham Harbour.

Tour 10

Around Chichester

Visit some of the historic houses, gardens and museums surrounding Chichester's sparkling harbour on this 36-mile (57km) driving tour

Chichester Harbour may be one of the smallest of Britain's Areas of Outstanding Natural Beauty, but it punches well above its weight. The wild, estuarine creeks, wind-sculpted woodlands and farms southwest of the cathedral city of Chichester are a haven for wildlife and wonderful to explore, with traces of Celtic, Roman and Saxon Britain close to the shore.

North of the city, the rolling hills of the South Downs National Park are dotted with historic sites and attractions. Those interested in hillforts, stately houses, gardens and the rich textures brought about by centuries of rural heritage will find plenty here to enjoy for a couple of days or more.

Highlights

- Chichester Harbour
- Fishbourne Roman Palace
- Stansted Park
- West Dean Gardens
- Weald and Downland Museum

CHICHESTER HARBOUR

Begin by treating yourself to a lungful of harbour air at **Itchenor ❶**, off the A286 southwest of Chichester. This quiet village is a focal point of the Chichester Harbour AONB (www.conservancy.co.uk), one of the few undeveloped coastal areas in southern England. A population of around 55,000 wildfowl including brent geese, dunlins and little egrets reside or winter on

Solar Heritage Boat Tours

Even if you're not a sailor, you can experience the peaceful waters of Chichester Harbour in an eco-friendly way on a short guided trip aboard Solar Heritage (Harbour Office, Itchenor; tel: 01243-513 275; www.conservancy.co.uk), a catamaran with solar panels on the roof. Stable, fume-free and almost silent, the boat skims across the water, making little wake and causing minimal disturbance to wildlife.

the AONB's mudflats, saltmarshes and dunes, and the surrounding countryside is crisscrossed by over 55 miles (90km) of public footpaths and cycle routes.

Itchenor lies on the Chichester Channel, one of the smooth fingers of water reaching inland from the main harbour on the Solent to the lowlands at the foot of the Downs. It's a dinghy sailors' hangout and the starting point for boat trips.

FISHBOURNE ROMAN PALACE

Retrace your route along the A286, then turn west along Dell Quay Road, north along Appledram Lane, west along the A259 and north to **Fishbourne**.

In the first century AD, the head of the Chichester Channel was the territory of Togidubnus, a British ruler who continued to reign after the Roman invasion. His sumptuous abode,

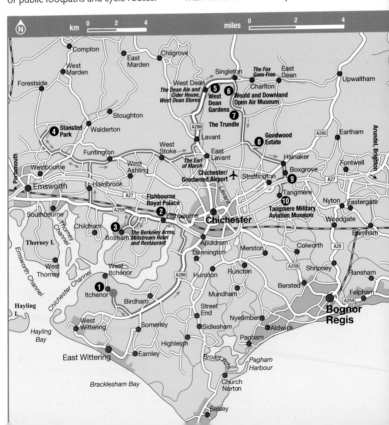

An elaborate mosaic at Fishbourne Royal Palace.

Fishbourne Royal Palace ❷ (tel: 01243-785 859; www.sussexpast. co.uk; Feb and Nov–Dec daily 10am–4pm, Mar–Oct daily 10am–5pm), is the largest surviving Roman-era domestic complex north of the Alps, with the most extensive collection of mosaics ever found in the UK.

The palace had more than 100 rooms graced with underfloor heating, indoor bathrooms and fabulous floors. Many of the remaining mosaics are highly ornate, with chalk-and-limestone geometrical patterns and motifs of mythical creatures including, famously, a cupid riding a dolphin. Destroyed by fire in 285 AD, the build-ing was lost to the world until 1960, when its remains were discovered by water mains engineers.

Artefacts, models, audiovisual displays and historical re-enactments bring everything to life. Horticultural archaeologists have worked out which plants Togidubnus' gardeners might have grown and briar, lavender and medicinal herbs have been planted, recreating one of the oldest gardens in England.

BOSHAM

Back on the A259, head west to Broadbridge then south along Delling Lane to the delightful harbourside village of **Bosham** ❸ (pronounced *Boz'm*). Out of season you can park on Shore Road, but beware the tide; it comes racing in to cover the tarmac, sometimes even lapping at doorways, which accounts for their flood defences.

The **Church of the Holy Trinity** has an idyllic waterfront location and is one of the oldest in Sussex; part Saxon, Norman and medieval, it contains masonry recycled from a Roman basilica. Its stout-walled tower, which features on the Bayeux Tapestry, sheltered women and children in times of

The Witterings

Blissfully undeveloped and sheltered, West Wittering is one of Sussex's few sandy beaches. Its enviable microclimate makes it ideal for picnics and paddling. Bracklesham Bay and East Wittering aren't as picturesque, but they appeal to fossil hunters: 45 million year old sharks' teeth and turtle shell fragments are sometimes found among the shingle.

Canute the Misunderstood

Thanks to the story of Canute ordering the waves to recede – supposedly on the shore at Bosham – popular legend paints him as a vainglorious king. However, the tale has been twisted over the years. According to the reliable 12th-century chronicler Henry of Huntingdon, Canute wasn't blowing his own trumpet at all, but reminding his overbearing courtiers that he was only human.

war. Later, when crusaders returned from the Holy Land, they blunted their sword tips on the stonework.

Bosham, an important medieval port, was one of the few places near Chichester where wine could be landed. In the black barn on the jetty, the **Raptackle**, tradesmen would make ropes, repair nets and sort oysters.

To round off your visit, drop into the **Anchor Bleu** pub (tel: 01243-573 956; www.anchorbleu.co.uk) or browse the **Bosham Walk Art and Craft Centre** (tel: 01243-572 475; www.bosham-walk.co.uk).

STANSTED PARK

Back on the A259, head west to Nutbourne, north via Hambrook to Common Road and west via Aldsworth to **Stansted Park ❹** (tel: 023-9241 2265; www.stanstedpark. co.uk; May–Sept Sun–Wed 1–5pm). This beautiful Restoration style mansion was built in 1901 to replace a hunting lodge that was destroyed by fire. The Edwardian owners took care to employ all the latest technology, including electric lighting, a panelled lift and garages instead of stables. The charitable foundation which now runs the estate have enhanced it with an eco-friendly biofuel boiler, fed with wood from Stansted's sustainable and biodiverse forest.

Beneath the elegant living rooms, the servants' quarters have been preserved as they would have been in the 1950s, complete with copper pots, mincers and the head butler's hand-written lists and accounts.

WEST DEAN

Retrace your route to Common Road, then continue east via the hamlets of Funtington, East Ashling, West Stoke and East Lavant to the A286,

The beach at West Wittering.

turning north towards Midhurst for West Dean.

The beautifully restored **West Dean Gardens** ❺ (tel: 01243-818 279; www.westdean.org.uk/gardens; daily Feb and Nov–Dec 10.30am–4pm, Mar–Oct 10.30am–5pm) feature Victorian hot houses, a walled kitchen garden, an arboretum and some unexpected sculptures. The estate belonged to the 20th-century art patron and eccentric Edward James, who had lobster-shaped telephones designed by Salvador Dalí in his mansion. Now West Dean College, it specialises in creative arts.

WEALD AND DOWNLOAD MUSEUM

Follow the A286 east for a mile, then, just before the pretty village of Singleton, turn south along Town Lane to the **Weald and Downland Open Air Museum** ❻ (tel: 01243-811 363; www.wealddown.co.uk; Jan–Feb Wed, Sat–Sun 10.30am–4pm, Mar and Nov–Dec daily 10.30am–4pm, Apr–Oct daily 10.30am–6pm).

This 50-acre (20-hectare) green swathe is been dotted with over 50

16th-century thatched cottage, Weald and Downland Open Air Museum.

historic buildings, rescued from all over southeast England. Spanning several centuries, the collection includes timber-framed cottages, thatched barns, shops, mills and a farmhouse which was uprooted from Kent during the building of the Eurotunnel terminal. Each was chosen for its distinctive rural character and some are filled with original artefacts, from tables to tools.

Throughout the year, volunteers offer demonstrations of traditional skills such as thatching, spinning, blacksmithing, Tudor cooking and garment-making. The museum also hosts lively events.

THE TRUNDLE

Continue south along Town Lane to The Triangle. A short walk up St Roche's Hill takes you to **The Trundle** ❼, an Iron Age hillfort built around 250 BC. It was the Celtic capital of the region until 50 BC and its present-day name is derived from the Saxon for circle, *tryndel*. The views from the top are magnificent, spanning the West Sussex Downs, Chichester Harbour and the Isle of Wight.

GOODWOOD

Continue south along Kennel Hill to the **Goodwood Estate** ❽ (tel:

Kingley Vale

The ancient yew forest in this National Nature Reserve is the largest and possibly the oldest in western Europe. Some of its trees are thought to be 2,000 years old; others were planted by Saxons to mark a victory against the marauding Danes. They survived the 15th century, when yews were felled to make longbows, and are now twisted with age, with a dense carpet of needles at their feet.

Festival of Speed hill course at Goodwood.

01243-755 055; www.goodwood. com), a chunk of downland which has been dedicated to sport since 1697 – first hunting, then cricket, horse racing, golf, motor racing and road cycling. These days, it's a big business with a trio of high-profile equestrian and motoring events: the Festival of Speed (June), Glorious Goodwood (July) and the Goodwood Revival (September). As well as its celebrated racecourse and golf courses, the estate boasts a luxury hotel, health club, flying school and organic farmshop.

Around 1.5 miles (2.5km) south of the racecourse is the entrance to **Goodwood House** (tel: 01243-927 332; www.goodwood.com; Mar–July and Sept–Oct Sun–Mon 1–5pm, Aug Sun–Thu 1–5pm), the lavishly furnished ancestral home of the Dukes of Richmond, Lennox, Gordon and Aubigny. Its state apartments gleam with treasures, from paintings by Canaletto, Stubbs and Reynolds to Sèvres porcelain, Gobelin tapestries and French furniture collected by the third duke when he was ambassador at the Versailles court of Louis XV.

Northeast of the mansion on New Barn Hill is the **Cass Sculpture Foundation** (tel: 01243-538 449; www.sculpture.org.uk; Apr–Oct daily 10.30am–4.30pm), an inspiring open air gallery of contemporary sculpture in gorgeous woods and parkland.

BOXGROVE AND TANGMERE

While it's a short drive back to Chichester from Goodwood, you might want to divert to **Boxgrove** ❾ to visit the **Tinwood Estate** (tel: 01243-537 372; www.tinwoodestate.com), a respected sparkling wine producer, and **Boxgrove Priory**, whose serene 12th-century Priory Church (www.boxgrovepriory.co.uk; daily until dusk) survived the dissolution of the monasteries and has beautiful 16th-century paintings on the ceiling and a modern stone labyrinth in the floor.

On the south side of the A27 from Boxgrove, the **Tangmere Military Aviation Museum** ❿ (tel: 01243-790 090; www.tangmere-museum. org; daily Feb and Nov 10am–4.30pm, Mar–Oct 10am–5pm) is a must for aviation enthusiasts. RAF Tangmere operated as a fighter aerodrome from 1917 to 1970 and was one of the Battle of Britain airfields. Among the planes on display is a Hawker Hunter, the last aircraft to fly from here.

Eating Out

Bosham

The Berkeley Arms

Bosham Lane; tel: 01243-573 167;
www.berkeleyarmsbosham.co.uk;
bar open Mon–Thu 11.30am–11pm,
Fri–Sat 11.30am–midnight, Sun noon–
11pm; food served Mon–Sat noon–
3pm and 6–9pm, Sun noon–6pm.
A down-to-earth village pub with real
ale on tap and good value pub classics
– whitebait, lasagne, lamb shank and
the like – on the menu. They often
run special offers such as steak, chips,
salad and wine for just £10. £££

Millstream Hotel and Restaurant

Bosham Lane; tel: 01243-573 234;
www.millstreamhotel.com; daily 7.30–
11.30am, 12.15–2pm and 6.30–9pm.
In a pretty terrace of 17th-century
cottages fronted by rose borders
and lawn, this hotel is open to non-
residents for hearty breakfasts and
elegant lunches and dinners, serving
dishes such as chicken terrine with
grape chutney, Thai green curry or
hake with chorizo. The dining room
has old-fashioned charm; there are
also tables in the garden. ££

West Dean and Charlton

The Dean Ale and Cider House

West Dean; tel: 01243-811 465;
www.thedeaninn.co.uk; bar open
Tue–Thu 11am–11pm, Fri–Sat
11am–midnight, Sun noon–10.30pm;
food served Tue–Sat 9–11.30am,
noon–3pm and 5.30–9.30pm, Sun
9–11.30am and noon–4pm.
If you fancy a chat about real ale, craft
beer and cider, this is the place – the
staff are passionate about British,
American and Belgian brews and
there's a blackboard covered with
tasting notes in the bar to prove it.
The restaurant is smart but unfussy,
with tasty seasonal pub classics to
match. Good value. ££

The Fox Goes Free

Charlton Road, Charlton; tel: 01243-
811 461; www.thefoxgoesfree.com;
bar open Mon–Sat 11am–11pm, Sun
noon–10.30pm; food served Mon–Fri
noon–2.30pm and 6.15–10pm, Sat
noon–10.30pm, Sun noon–5pm and
6.15–9.30pm.
This triumphantly named pub can
trace its history back 400 years. Its
higgledy-piggledy rooms are packed
with charm, with old timbers and
crackling fires. The menu features
classics like fish pie, steak, and
honey-roasted gammon. ££

West Dean Stores

West Dean; tel: 01243-818 163;
www.westdeanstores.co.uk; Mon
8am–5.30pm, Tue 8am–1pm,
Wed–Fri 8am–5.30pm, Sat 8.30am–
4.30pm, Sun 8.30am–1pm.
Every village should have a shop like
this – small but cute and packed with
local produce and essentials. Best of
all, West Dean Stores has a cosy tea
room where you can eavesdrop on
all the gossip over tea or coffee and
bacon baps, scones or ice cream. £

Lavant

The Earl of March

Lavant Road, Lavant; tel: 01243-533
993; www.theearlofmarch.com; bar
open Mon–Fri 11am–11pm, Sat 11am–
11.30pm, Sun 11am–10.30pm; food
served Mon–Sat noon–2.30pm and
5.30–9pm, Sun noon–3pm and 6–9pm.
This country pub has a cosy fireside
bar area, a smart dining room and a
garden with wonderful views of fields
and trees. The food is classy but
good value, especially at lunchtime
and before 7pm, with a choice of
light dishes such as salads or battered
fish and specialities such as wild sea
trout with clams or roast breast of
guineafowl. ££

Petworth House.

Tour 11

Midhurst and Around

This 16-mile (25km) drive takes in the pretty market town of Midhurst and some of the finest country houses in West Sussex

The northern reaches of West Sussex have a distinctly aristocratic air. Less than 60 miles (97km) from London and within easy reach of Southampton, Portsmouth and Chichester, this region is graced by several handsome country estates. The grandest is without a doubt Petworth House, which contains an outstanding collection of paintings, sculpture and decorative carvings.

The Rother Valley has been a crossroads for travellers and traders since Saxon times. The town of Midhurst was already thriving at the time of the Norman invasion and flourished in the centuries that followed. Now part of the South Downs National Park, its surroundings retain their rural charm, with winding lanes and ancient timber cottages.

Highlights

- Uppark House
- Midhurst
- Cowdray Park
- Petworth House

UPPARK HOUSE

Start your tour at **Uppark House** ❶ (South Harting; tel: 01730-825 857; www.nationaltrust.org.uk/uppark; house: Mar–Oct Wed–Sun 12.30–4.30pm, Nov–Feb Sat–Sun noon–3pm; servants quarters: Mar–Oct daily 11am–4.30pm, Nov–Feb daily 11am–3pm; gardens: daily 10am–5pm). This neat-fronted, late 17th-century mansion, designed to conform to the Georgian ideals of symmetry and proportion, perches on a ridge amid sweeping lawns and wildflower meadows. The front of the house has spectacular views of the West Sussex countryside, with the Solent and Portsmouth's Spinnaker Tower in the distance.

Uppark, which was ruined by fire in 1989, was one of the National Trust's greatest ever restoration projects. The interior illustrates the divide between Regency aristocrats and their servants, with the upstairs rooms lavishly decorated with chandeliers, panelling and a Grand Tour collection of paintings and the downstairs rooms given over to a spartan kitchen, pantry and stores. The whole ensemble is echoed in a genuine Regency doll's house.

MIDHURST

Next, drive around 8 miles (13km) northeast to the sleepy but appealing town of **Midhurst** ❷. Its small, medieval Market Square has been used for trading for over 500 years and is still very much the heart of town. Bordering the square is the Church of St Mary Magdalene and St Denys, founded by the Normans, and a jumble of historic buildings, one of which has served

Petworth Antiques

Petworth is a treasure trove of antique shops, with Lombard Street, a narrow cobbled lane leading off the Market Square, the heart of the action. Just round the corner on East Street is Petworth Antiques Market (tel: 01798-343 178; www.petworth antiquecentre.co.uk) which houses over 30 dealers selling everything from rare books, furniture and garden ornaments to needlepoint samplers and ladies' fans.

as a market hall and town hall. Until 1859, miscreants used to be clapped in stocks outside. The Spread Eagle Hotel on South Street, nearby, hosted the Pilgrim Fathers in 1620 and Admiral Lord Nelson in the 1790s.

Midhurst is home to the South Downs Centre (North Street; 01730-814 810; www.southdowns.gov.uk; Mon–Thu 9am–5pm, Fri 9am–4.30pm, Sat 10.30am–2.30pm), the modern, eco-friendly head office and information centre for the South Downs National Park.

The market town of Midhurst.

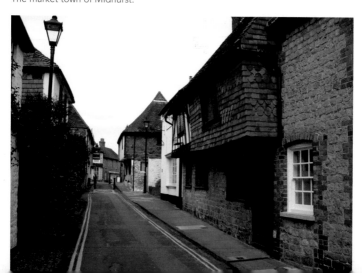

The ruins of Cowdray House.

COWDRAY

Follow North Street (A286/A272) north across the River Rother and turn right at the roundabout to enter the **Cowdray Estate** ❸ (www. cowdray.co.uk). This impressive country property contains the gaunt Cowdray House Ruins (www.cowdray. org.uk; Mar–Oct Mon–Thu and Sun 10.30am–5pm), the remains of an important early Tudor manor house. Second in size to Hampton Court in the 16th century, the building was ruined by fire in 1793, supposedly fulfilling a 250-year-old curse.

A century after the fire, the estate's former keeper's lodge on the edge of the village of Easebourne was remodelled as a substantial mansion, Cowdray Park House, which became the owners' home. It's recently been renamed Cowdray House (www. cowdrayhouse.co.uk), rather confusingly, and is available to hire for private events. New additions include a farm shop and café.

The beautiful walled garden adjacent to the ruins is now a wedding venue and a variety of summer events are held on the estate, which contains a golf course and one of Britain's best known polo grounds.

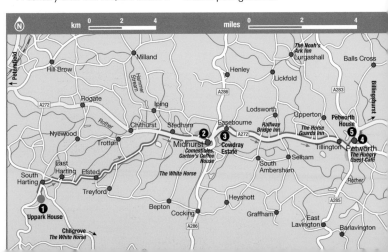

Burton Mill Pond

Three miles south of Petworth, an old water mill overlooks a 16th-century hammer pond, the Sussex term for a small lake created by diverting the course of several brooks to power the massive hammer and bellows of a forge. Today, this is a tranquil spot to look for dragonflies, kingfishers or great crested grebes.

PETWORTH

Return to the A272 and continue around 5.5 miles east to **Petworth ❹**. This attractive little town suffers from its lack of a bypass but has plenty of charm, with a market square surrounded by Georgian-fronted buildings and antique shops.

Petworth is dominated by the Leconfield Estate and its manor, Petworth House, on which it depends. At the delightful Petworth Cottage Museum (346 High Street; www. petworthcottagemuseum.co.uk; Apr–Oct Tue–Sat 2–4.30pm) you can get a feel for the way estate workers lived in the early 20th century. If you follow the High Street into Grove Street, you'll find several pretty terraces of 19th-century workers' cottages with brown front doors, each marked with

a number corresponding to Lord Leconfield's rent records.

PETWORTH HOUSE

On the north side of Petworth in a vast deer park landscaped by Capability Brown, **Petworth House ❺** (tel: 01798-343 929; www.national trust.org.uk/petworth; grounds daily 10am–5.30pm; house Mar–Oct daily 11am–5pm) is one of Britain's most celebrated stately homes.

You approach through gardens dotted with specimen trees and enter via a courtyard that separates the servants' quarters from the main house. Built in the late 17th century, the house has a simple, clean Regency facade that does little to prepare you for the riches within. The elaborately decorated state rooms contain a breathtaking collection of paintings and neoclassical sculpture, including works by Turner, Titian, Gainsborough, Van Dyck, Reynolds and Blake.

The biggest surprise is the Carved Room, adorned with intricate wood carvings of musical instruments, cherubs and garlands of leaves and fruit. They're the work of the 17th-century master carver Grinling Gibbons. The kitchen is also quite a scene-stealer, impressive in scale, with a gleaming copper batterie de cuisine of more than 1,000 pieces.

Petworth Park.

Eating Out

Chilgrove
The White Horse
1 High Street; tel: 01243-519 444;
www.thewhitehorse.co.uk; food
served Mon–Fri 8am–10am, noon–
2.30pm and 6–9.30pm, Sat–Sun
8am–10am and noon–9.30pm.
The White Horse offers excellent pub
fare and welcomes its guests with
thoughtful touches, from the jar of
dog biscuits on the bar to the stash of
reading glasses for those who keep
forgetting their own. Take a table in
the garden with peaceful farmland
views or snuggle into a leather
armchair by the wood-burner. ££

Midhurst
Comestibles
Red Lion Street; tel: 01730-813 400;
www.picnic-park.co.uk; Mon–Sat
8am–5pm.
Passionate about food, the owners of
Midhurst's deli and community café
create picnic hampers for people
attending the region's many outdoor
events. You could put together your
own delicious takeaway lunch or enjoy
a salad or coffee on the spot. £

Garton's Coffee House
Market Square; tel: 01730-817 166;
www.gartons.net; daily 8.30am–
4.30pm.
The pretty square outside Garton's is
a lovely place to relax on a sunny day,
with fine views of the church and its
yew-shaded churchyard. This licensed
café, housed in the old Town Hall,
serves full English breakfasts, light
lunches and tasty afternoon treats. £

Lurgashall, Lodsworth and Tillington
Halfway Bridge Inn
Halfway Bridge, Lodsworth; tel:
01798-344 564; www.halfwaybridge.
co.uk; food served Mon–Fri noon–
2pm and 6–9pm, Sat–Sun noon–9pm.

This pleasant 17th-century pub with
rooms has been gently modernised
but retains its parquet floors and
open fires. British and Mediterranean-
inspired gourmet fare such as roasted
salmon fillet with caper butter or rump
of lamb with charred courgettes,
pancetta and Madeira jus. £££

The Horse Guards Inn
Upperton Road, Tillington; tel: 01798-
342 332; www.thehorseguardsinn.
co.uk; food served Mon–Thu
noon–2.30pm and 6.30–9pm, Fri
noon–2.30pm and 6–9.30pm, Sat
noon–3pm and 6.30–9.30pm, Sun
noon–3.30pm and 6.30–9pm.
This friendly, quirky pub serves good,
honest food made from produce
bought or foraged locally. Some
ingredients come from the back
garden, home to hens, tomato plants
and tubs of herbs. On sunny days,
there's outdoor seating on benches
and rug-covered straw bales. £££

The Noah's Ark Inn
The Green, Lurgashall; tel: 01428-707
346; www.noahsarkinn.co.uk; food
served Mon–Sat noon–2.30pm and
7–9.30pm, Sun noon–3.15pm.
If relaxing with a pint to the sound of
leather on willow is your idea of bliss,
you'll love Noah's Ark. It has outdoor
tables right beside the cricket pitch
and a bright, welcoming dining room
serving fresh, modern food. Local
ingredients including eggs from the
landlord's own flock. ££

Petworth
The Hungry Guest Café
Lombard Street; tel: 01798-344 564;
www.thehungryguest.com; Mon–Sat
9am–6pm, Sun 9am–5pm.
Excellent value breakfasts, artisan
coffee, sourdough pizzas, sandwiches,
salads and more. Kids' portions
available. £

View of Arundel Castle from the River Arun.

Tour 12

Arundel and Around

Take a stroll around the elegant fortified town of Arundel then head north on a 16-mile (25km) driving tour of the surrounding countryside

warfed by its hilltop castle and soaring Neo-Gothic Catholic cathedral, the handsome market town of Arundel gazes out over the winding River Arun. It was mentioned as a river port in the Domesday Book and its busy quay, fish market and customs house remained active until the 19th century, when Littlehampton superseded it.

These days, the town is a pleasant place to wander, with antique shops to browse and cricket matches and other events to enjoy in the castle grounds. In the swathe of parklands north of the castle, there's the picturesque Swanbourne Lake and the WWT Arundel Wetland Centre to explore. Beyond, the Arun Valley brims with West Sussex charm.

Highlights

- Arundel Castle
- Arundel Wetland Centre
- Bignor Roman Villa
- Amberley
- Parham House and Gardens

ARUNDEL

Start your stroll around **Arundel ❶** at the Crown Yard car park opposite the Lower Castle Gate on Mill Road. Near the entrance, **Arundel Museum** (tel: 01903-885 866; www.arundelmuseum.org; daily 10am–4pm), an attractive modern building with brick and flint walls, offers tourist information and a wealth of knowledge on local folklore and heritage. If

Arundel Lido

How many open-air swimming pools can boast a view of a castle? Little ones can bathe like knights and princesses at the Arundel Lido (Queen Street; tel: 01903-884 772; www.arundel-lido.com; May–Aug Mon–Fri noon–7pm, Sat–Sun and school holidays 10am–7pm), which has a 25-metre pool, two kids' pools and picnic lawns. The backdrop may make you gasp, but the water won't – it's heated to a pleasant 28°C.

An inquisitive swan on the River Arun, near Arundel.

you're curious about what the Knucker Hole might be or why the local football team are known as The Mullets, you'll find the answers here.

Arundel Castle
Arundel Castle (tel: 01903-882 173; www.arundelcastle.org; Easter–Oct Tue–Sun and bank holidays 10am–5pm), one of England's finest, has belonged to the powerful Dukes of Norfolk, England's senior Roman Catholic family, since the 16th century.

Much of the present-day structure is far younger than it looks – it underwent major rebuilding and restoration work in the 19th century – but there has been a fort here since Saxon times. In the 12th century, Roger de Montgomery replaced it with a sturdy stone castle, but this was virtually destroyed by Oliver Cromwell's Parliamentarians during the Civil War.

The oldest surviving section is the Norman keep, built in 1190. Its steep stairs lead you to glorious views of Arundel, the Downs and the coast. There are also state rooms to visit, including a huge Barons' Hall and richly furnished dining and drawing rooms, stuffed with tapestries and treasures.

Arundel town centre
West of the Lower Castle Gate, head uphill through Arundel's compact historic centre. As you follow the High Street north, you'll pass plenty of appealing cafés, antique merchants and independent shops.

From the Tudor-style **Post Office** on the corner of Mill Road to the Norman-style **Town Hall** on Maltravers Street, many of Arundel's prominent buildings are, like the castle, 19th-century imitations of earlier architectural styles. There's a wealth

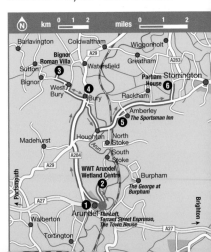

of detail to admire, such as the street lamps on Maltravers Street, which hark back to the days of gas lighting.

Bristling with spiky stone adornments, **Arundel Cathedral** (London Road; tel: 01903-882 297; www.arundelcathedral.org; daily 9am–6pm) is one of Britain's most impressive French Gothic style buildings. Commissioned by the 15th Duke of Norfolk in the 1870s as a gift to the Catholics of Sussex, its design evokes the 1300s, the era his ancestors first rose to prominence. It's famous for its Corpus Christi celebrations in June, when the aisle is carpeted with flowers.

Also on London Road is the 14th-century **Church of St Nicholas and Fitzalan Chapel** (tel: 01903-882 262; www.stnicholas-arundel.co.uk). Uniquely, it's dual-purpose. While the nave is an Anglican parish church, the chancel, separated by an iron and glass screen and only accessible via the castle, is Catholic, and contains the tombs of the earls of Arundel.

WWT ARUNDEL WETLAND CENTRE

From the Lower Castle Gate, a leafy avenue leads north to **Swanbourne**

Listening for Birds

Each season brings new bird calls to the Sussex countryside. In spring, lapwings and oystercatchers whoop and squeak in wetland areas and country lanes come alive with the high-pitched calls of great tits. Summer downland walks are made magical by the virtuoso singing of skylarks; head into the woods to catch chaffinches and warblers trilling over the staccato hammering of woodpeckers. Once the summer migrants move on, you'll still hear jackdaws chattering from village trees and robins whistling bright tunes.

Lake, where there are rowing boats for hire (Mar–Oct), and the **WWT Arundel Wetland Centre ❷** (Mill Road; tel: 01903-883 355; www.wwt.org.uk/wetland-centres/arundel; daily Apr–mid-Oct 9.30am–5.30pm, mid-Oct–Mar 9.30am–4.30pm), which protects a lush network of reedy channels and wildflower meadows beside the River Arun. This scenic reserve, framed by rolling downland scenery, is easy to explore on foot. With bird seed to buy,

Arundel Cathedral.

A pheasant amid cowslips at the WWT Arundel Wetland Centre.

a pond-dipping station and eight hides including a family-friendly one with a child-sized telescope, there's plenty to keep young naturalists busy.

Ducks, geese, grebes, swans and other water-loving birds congregate here, and dragonflies and butterflies brighten the views from the walkways. Included in the entry fee is a short tour in a small, open electric boat that glides along quietly enough to let you enjoy the birdsong. The sharp-eared may even hear water voles munching on shoots.

Half a mile (0.6km) northeast is the **Black Rabbit** (Mill Road; tel: 01903-882 828; www.theblackrabbitarundel. co.uk), a country pub with an unbeatable riverside setting, right on a bend in the Arun. While its food is basic, it's an idyllic spot for a drink.

BIGNOR ROMAN VILLA

Head north out of Arundel via the A284 and A29, signposted to Pulborough. At the top of Bury Hill, turn west along Westburton Lane to **Bignor Roman Villa ❸** (tel: 01798-869 259; www.bignorromanvilla.

co.uk; Mar–Oct daily 10am–5pm). Built in the first century AD, this substantial Roman farmhouse was demolished a couple of centuries later and forgotten until 1811, when a local farmer hit a foundation stone with his plough.

Excavation soon followed, revealing some of Britain's most intact mosaic floors. Superbly detailed, they depict cherubs, gladiators, Venus and Medusa and are sheltered by a cluster of 1820s thatched cottages. It's thought that the original villa contained well over 60 rooms.

South of Bignor and West Burton is a peaceful, breezy stretch of the South Downs Way with spectacular Arun Valley views from Westburton Hill and Bury Hill.

AMBERLEY

Return to the A29 and cross it to drive through the pretty village of **Bury ❹**, home in the 1920s to Nobel Prize winning author John Galsworthy. Follow Houghton Lane south, then at Houghton head east along the B2139, following and then crossing the River

Amberley Castle.

Arun at **Amberley ❺**, one of the most delightful villages in Sussex.

Just beyond the railway station is the popular and successful **Amberley Museum and Heritage Centre** (tel: 01798-831 370; www.amberleymuseum.co.uk; Mar–Oct Wed–Sun 10am–5pm; daily during school holidays). It's principally an open-air museum, featuring a narrow gauge railway, lime kilns, a brickmaking works and a blacksmith's forge, with craftworkers on hand to demonstrate traditional skills.

The heart of the village, a mile (1.6km) further north, is a mellow jumble of thatched cottages, with a lane leading to **Amberley Village Pottery** (tel: 01798-831 876; www.amberleypottery.co.uk; Thu–Tue 11am–3pm), the 12th-century **Church of St Michael** and **Amberley Castle**, a medieval manor ringed by 14th-century stone fortifications. Originally a palace for the bishops of Chichester, it's now a hotel. To the north, the **Wildbrooks** water meadows beside the River Arun are an important breeding site for birds and a picture of peace.

PARHAM HOUSE AND GARDENS

From Amberley, follow the B2139 east towards Storrington, turning left after

The Glasshouse at Parham House.

2 miles (3km) to visit one of the finest Elizabethan mansions in England, **Parham House ❻** (near Pulborough; tel: 01903-742 021; www.parhamin sussex.co.uk; Easter–Sept Wed–Fri, Sun and bank holidays; house 2–5pm, gardens noon–5pm).

A corruption of 'pear homestead', the Parham estate was originally a farm supplying Westminster Abbey. The house, which is immaculately presented, was built in 1577 and only three families have lived here since. Its wonderful grounds include an orchard, walled gardens and a landscaped, biodiversity-friendly park.

Eating Out

Arundel
The Loft
Sparks Yard, 18 Tarrant Street; tel: 01903-885 588; www.sparksyard. com; Mon–Sat 9.30am–5.30pm, Sun 10am–5pm.
Whether you're after pancakes with bacon and maple syrup for breakfast, a burger with Monterey Jack cheese for lunch or a teatime chocolate and banana sundae, The Loft hits the spot. It's an airy, Californian-style café with a fresh, modern feel. £

The George at Burpham
Main Street, Burpham; tel: 01903-883 131; www.georgeatburpham.co.uk; bar open Mon–Fri 10.30am–3pm and 6–11pm, Sat 10.30am–11pm, Sun 10.30am–10pm; food served Mon–Fri noon–2.30pm and 6–9pm, Sat noon–3pm and 6–9.30pm, Sun noon– 5pm (winter), noon–4pm and 6–8.30pm (summer).
Owned by a group of local residents, this friendly country pub offers excellent food featuring West Sussex produce. Hearty pub classics to choose from include beer battered cod, slow-roasted pork belly and fillet steak. Families, walkers, cyclists and dog walkers are made very welcome. ££

Tarrant Street Espresso
17 Tarrant Street; tel: 01903-885 350; Tue–Fri 7.30am–4pm, Sat–Sun 9am–4pm.

This tiny independent coffee bar serves expertly selected and prepared coffee to enjoy solo or with a savoury roll, chocolate chip cookie, muffin or slab of cake. It's great for a quick take-away and there are a few stools to perch on, too. £

The Town House
65 High Street; tel: 01903-883 847; www.thetownhouse.co.uk; Tue–Sat noon–2.30pm and 6–9pm.
The first thing you do on entering the dining room of this smart little Regency restaurant with rooms is look up – the walnut ceiling, elaborately gilded, is extraordinary. Carved in Florence in the 16th century, it was installed when the house was built in the early 1800s. Expect modern bistro-style food using local ingredients such as pigeon, venison and scallops. £££

Amberley
The Sportsman Inn
Rackham Road; tel: 01798-831 787; www.thesportsmanamberley.com; bar open Mon–Sat 11am–11pm, Sun noon–10.30pm; food served Mon–Sat noon–2.30pm and 6.30–9pm, Sun noon–5pm and 6.30–9pm.
This pub has won several CAMRA awards for the quality of its real ale, with several local brews always on tap. Simple, tasty lunches and suppers are cooked on the premises and walkers can order a packed lunch to take away. £

The Royal Pavilion.

Beachy Head.

Travel Tips

Active Pursuits

From windsurfing to wildlife-watching, Sussex has a host of activities to keep you occupied. Whatever your interests, the South Downs National Park headquarters in Midhurst, city tourist information offices and nature reserve visitor centres can help with brochures, maps and advice.

Ordnance Survey Landranger map 197 (Chichester and the South Downs), 198 (Brighton and Lewes), 199 (Eastbourne and Hastings) are excellent for planning, while the larger scale 1:25,000 maps from the OS Explorer series are invaluable for indicating details such as footpaths, bridleways, campsites and pubs. OS Explorer maps are available in printed or digital form at www.ordnancesurvey.co.uk.

WALKING AND HIKING

Historic city streets, woodland paths, downland trails and coastal tracks with fabulous sea views make Sus-sex a great place to stretch your legs. There's proper countryside to be found within easy reach of the main towns, but wherever you wander, you're never too far from the nearest pub or teashop.

In total, the South Downs National Park (www.southdowns.gov.uk) has around 2,000 miles (3,300km) of footpaths and the High Weald Area of Outstanding Natural Beauty (www.highweald.org) has some 1,500 miles (2,400km). Both have mapped many walks of varying lengths, published as leaflets and available to download from their websites. Some walks are linked into waymarked trails such as the Centurion Way (Chichester to West Dean), the Vanguard Way (Croydon to Newhaven) and the High Weald Landscape Trail (Horsham to Rye).

The best known of the region's long-distance footpaths is the South Downs Way (www.nationaltrail.co.uk/

A signpost guides walkers along the South Downs Way.

south-downs-way), an epic 100-mile (160km) walk from Winchester to Eastbourne which is enjoyable in either direction. Undulating and occasionally muddy but otherwise undemanding, it immerses you in glorious scenery, from rolling farmland, leafy woodland and wildflower glades to the open, grassy slopes cresting the Downs.

You don't need to commit to walking the whole route. There are small car parks, villages, bus stops and railway stations nearby, making it easy to dip in and out, whether you fancy a full day's hike or simply a quick ramble to work up an appetite for lunch. A handy public transport map and a list of car parks are available to download from the South Downs Way website.

If you'd like to make walking the focus of your trip, good bases to choose include Amberley, which has a railway station and is surrounded by fine scenery, and Alfriston, a beautiful, historic village at a junction of the South Downs Way.

CYCLING

Sussex has much to offer both road cyclists and mountain bikers. The terrain is satisfyingly varied, with everything from smooth, flat seafront cycle paths to gnarly downland tracks.

Traffic can be fast-moving, even on the tiniest country lanes, so the safest bet is to stick to cycle paths and bridleways. The 100-mile (160km) South Downs Way runs right the way across the South Downs National Park and is the only one of Britain's National Trails that is fully traversable by bike. You could tackle the whole thing in two to four days – or just one, if you're super-fit. For an online map showing cycle hire and repair shops, water points and other essential information, visit www.nationaltrail.co.uk/south-downs-way/plan.

Other trails to explore include the Centurion Way, a 5-mile (8km) cycling and walking route from Chichester to West Dean, the 5-mile (8km) Salterns Way from Chichester to West Wittering and the 14-mile (23km) Cuckoo Trail from Heathfield to Hampden Park, which is surfaced and follows an old railway route.

To really test your mettle, you could head for a mountain bike and BMX hotspot such as Steyning MTB, Shore-

Cycling along the Cuckoo Trail, which runs from Heathfield to Hampden Park.

ham Dirt Jumps, Sidley Woods in Bex-hill or Friston Forest near East Dean.

Most cities and towns in Sussex have places where you can hire a bicycle for anything from a couple of hours to several weeks, or get your own machine serviced.

BEACHES AND SWIMMING

Brighton and Hove's long pebbly shore is arguably the best city beach in Britain, and there are appealing pebble beaches at Bognor Regis, Climping, Littlehampton, Cuckmere Haven, Eastbourne, Pevensey and Hastings. For glorious sandy dunes, head for West Wittering or Camber Sands. Between May and September, lifeguards patrol flagged sections of the most popular beaches.

While nobody would pretend that the English Channel is ever truly warm – the temperature peaks in late August at around 19°C (66°F) – a dip on a summer day can be truly invigorating. Aqua shoes make it easier to deal with the pebbles. Some hardy souls swim in the sea on calm days all year round, donning wetsuits when it's chilly. However, it's crucial to be cautious in areas where the pebbles slope steeply and to stay away when conditions are rough, as serious accidents can happen even when paddling.

Brighton Beach.

Get Wet and Go Wild

If your kids love hurtling down waterslides, they'll adore the Fun Pool at Eastbourne's Sovereign Centre, which has a flume, waves and a water cannon. There's also a 25-metre gala pool and a diving pool in the complex. Splashpoint in Worthing has a flume and an outdoor paddling pool for water babies to splash about in, while Chichester's Westgate Leisure Centre has a 55-metre water slide and an indoor play pool for toddlers.

For a freshwater swim, try Chichester Watersports (tel: 01243-776 349; www.chichesterwatersports.co.uk) on Westhampnett Lake, just outside Chichester, or Barcombe Mills on the River Ouse, north of Lewes.

LIDOS AND LEISURE CENTRES

The most attractive public lidos in the region covered by this book include the Pells Pool in Lewes (see page 56) and Arundel Lido (see page 105). Funds have been raised to renovate Saltdean's attractive Art Deco lido; it's hoped it will re-open in 2016.

Kayaking along the River Cuckmere.

The best leisure centres with swimming pools include Bexhill (tel: 01424-731 508; www.freedom-leisure.co.uk), King Alfred (Hove; tel: 01273-290 290; www.freedom-leisure.co.uk), Lewes (tel: 01273-486 000; www.waveleisure.co.uk), Splashpoint (Worthing; tel: 01903-905 050; www.south-downsleisure.co.uk), Sovereign (Eastbourne; tel: 01323-738 822; www.eastbourneleisurecentres.com) and Westgate (Chichester; tel: 01243-785 651; www.westgateleisure.co.uk).

WATERSPORTS

Chichester, Brighton and Eastbourne are major coastal watersports hubs, with busy marinas. RYA courses in yachting, dinghy sailing and powerboating are available at Chichester Sea School (Chichester Marina; tel 07836-221 930; www.chichesterseaschool.com), the Sussex Yacht Club (Shoreham-by-Sea; tel: 01273-464 868 www.sussexyachtclub.org.uk), Sea Training Sussex (Eastbourne Marina; tel: 07713-639 066; www.seatrainingsussex.co.uk) and Waterfront Sailing (Brighton Marina; tel: 01273-818 154; www.waterfrontsailing.com), which also offers bare boat and skippered boat charters.

On Hove seafront, Lagoon Watersports (Hove Lagoon; tel: 01273-424 842; www.lagoon.co.uk) offers windsurfing, wakeboarding and stand-up paddleboarding instruction in safe, shallow water. The open sea nearby is a favourite spot for windsurfers and kitesurfers to try out their moves.

West Sussex has a freshwater venue, Westhampnett Lake, where Chichester Watersports (tel: 01243-776 349; www.chichesterwatersports.co.uk) runs windsurfing, wakeboarding, stand-up paddleboarding, waterskiing and kayaking courses with all the kit you'll need. In East Sussex, you can canoe on the idyllic Cuckmere River with the Cuckmere Valley Canoe Club (www.cvcc.org.uk).

For those keen to explore between the surface, scuba diving training and trips are available at Chichester Sub Aqua Club (tel: 07557-361 149; www.chichestersac.com), Oyster Diving (Brighton; tel: 07920-516 006; www.oysterdiving.com), Planet Divers (Eastbourne; tel: 07889-883 232; www.planetdivers.co.uk) and the Sussex Yacht Club in Shoreham.

Horse riders on the South Downs.

HORSE RIDING

Sussex is a hugely enjoyable place to ride, with around 750 miles (1,200km) of bridleways in the South Downs National Park alone, some of which follow historic drovers' trails over the chalk downlands. With the exception of the Cuckmere Haven loop south of Alfriston, which is for walkers only, the entire 100-mile (160km) South Downs Way from Winchester to Eastbourne is a bridleway. It's advisable to skip the westernmost section between Chilcomb and Winchester though, in order to avoid the city centre and the M3 crossing. For an online map of the South Downs Way showing stables, horsebox parking, tack shops, water points and other essential information, visit www.national trail.co.uk/south-downs-way/plan.

Outside the national park, there are trails to explore in Ashdown Forest; to ride here, you need to obtain a permit from the Ashdown Forest Centre (Wych Cross; tel: 01342-823 583; www.ashdownforest.org). Alternatively, to feel the sea breeze on your face, you could ride on the beach at Pevensey Bay or West Wittering.

Long-distance riding is a great way to experience the outdoors and really bond with your horse; you can expect to cover 30 miles (48km) in a full day's ride at easy walking pace. B&Bs in the South Downs National Park which accept horses as well as riders include Willow Barns (Graffham; tel: 01798-867 493; www.willowbarns.co.uk) and The Paddocks (Jevington; tel: 01323-482 499; www.thepaddockstables. co.uk). Options in the High Weald include Adds Farm (near Crowborough; tel: 01892-231 361; www.holidays withyourhorse.co.uk), Moss Cottage (near Wych Cross; 01342-823 913; www.mosscottagebandb.co.uk)

For beginners, improvers and those who don't have their own horse, Sussex has plenty of stables and riding schools which offer lessons and tours. For details of approved riding centres, contact the British Horse Society (www.bhs.org.uk) and the Association of British Riding Schools (www. abrs-info.org).

When riding in rural Sussex, it's important to be considerate of walkers, local farmers and their livestock, watch out for dogs and avoid jumping hedgerows or fallen timber. Make sure you also remove your horse's droppings and straw from parking areas.

WILDLIFE, NATURE AND BUSHCRAFT

With a rich variety of habitats including woodlands, wetlands and down-

Geocaching

Like a high-tech treasure hunt, geocaching (www.geocaching.com) takes you on a trail of discovery. You use a GPS or smartphone app to locate hidden boxes, each containing a log book and sometimes a token prize. It's a fun idea for a day out. For details of a 30-point geocaching trail in the South Downs National Park, search for GeoTour at www.south downs.gov.uk.

lands, Sussex is excellent for bird-watching, tree spotting and bug hunts. The National Trust (tel: 0844-800 1895; www.nationaltrust.org.uk) and Sussex Wildlife Trust (tel: 01273-497 561; www.sussexwildlifetrust.org.uk) organise nature walks and activities on a regular basis.

Families yearning to bond with nature will find masses of inspiration in the activities organised by So Sussex (tel: 07739-050 816; www.sosussex. co.uk), including foraging, story-telling and wild camping. They also run Elderflower Fields (www.elderflower fields.co.uk), a family weekend festival held in Pippingford Park near Wych Cross in May.

Paragliding over the scenic Devil's Dyke valley.

For adults, Plumpton's highly respected sustainable agriculture and forestry centre, Plumpton College (www. plumpton.ac.uk), offers short courses in traditional skills such as floristry, metalsmithing and making trugs (Sussex baskets of chestnut and willow). In Midhurst, John Rhyder's Woodcraft School (tel: 01730-816 299; www. woodcraftschool.co.uk) can teach you to identify fungi, medicinal plants and wildlife, or give you a grounding in survival skills.

PARAGLIDING

Experts consider the South Downs one of the world's finest and safest paragliding spots, even in winter. To learn the ropes, contact Airworks (Glynde; tel: 01273-434 002; www. airworks.co.uk) or Fly Sussex (Toll-gate; tel: 01273-858 170; www.fly sussex.com).

Place Your Bets

Held over five days in July, Glorious Goodwood (tel: 01243-755 055; www.goodwood.com) is one of the highlights of the British flat racing calendar. Though not as posh as Royal Ascot, Ladies' Day attracts a colourful crowd in smart summer suits and big hats. For other opportunities to watch some equestrian action, look out for racing fixtures at Brighton (tel: 01273-603 580; www.brighton-racecourse. co.uk), Plumpton (tel: 01273-890 383; www.plumptonracecourse.co.uk) or Fontwell Park (tel: 01243-543 335; www.fontwellpark.co.uk). Horse trials are held at Borde Hill (tel: 01323-440 003; www.bordehillhorsetrials. com), Brightling Park (tel: 01424-838 241; www.brightlinghorsetrials.co.uk) and Firle Place (tel: 01323-482 016; www.firleplaceevent.co.uk).

Themed Holidays

From energetic cycling trips to relaxing painting courses, there's a wide variety of activity holidays on offer in Sussex.

WALKING AND CYCLING

Several specialist holiday companies offer guided or self-guided walking and cycling breaks in Sussex. You can choose between group tours with a fixed itinerary, or tailor-made trips which allow you to set your own distance and pace.

The South Downs Way is perfect for point-to-point walks and mountain bike rides, staying in B&Bs and using a baggage transfer service, so the most you need carry each day is a daypack. Footprints of Sussex (tel: 01903-813 381; www.footprintsofsussex.co.uk), based in Steyning, have a wealth of local knowledge. As well as offering bespoke trips, they organise a nine-day group walk along the South Downs Way each June. Starting from Winchester in even years and Eastbourne in odd years, it's broken into legs of around 11 miles (18km). The Footprints team recommends accommodation and provides daily coach transfers.

National activity holiday companies such as Contours (tel: 01629-821 900; www.contours.co.uk), HF Holidays (tel: 0345-470 8558; www.hfholidays. co.uk), Celtic Trails (tel: 01291-689 774; www.celtic-trails.com) and Walk & Cycle (tel: 0844-870 8648; www. walkandcycle.co.uk) also run South Downs trips. Country Walks (tel: 020-7233 6563; www.country-walks.com) offers self-guided downland and coastal walking holidays from Alfriston.

HORSE RIDING

Equestrian centres offering riding holidays in Sussex include Hurstwood Farm (Hurstwood, near Uckfield; tel: 01825-732 002; www.equestriantrain ingcentre.co.uk), which has affordable accommodation in a converted barn. It's also possible to ride independently, booking B&Bs with stables and using a baggage transfer service such as South Downs Discovery (tel: 01925-

Walking on the South Downs.

564 475; www.southdownsdiscovery. com) to carry your luggage and supplies from one to the next.

GLAMPING, WILDLIFE AND NATURE

Posh camping allows you to immerse yourself in the countryside while sleeping in something far more interesting than a basic tent.

The Shepherd's Hut (Standean Farm, Patcham; tel: 01273-501 469; www.the-shepherds-hut.co.uk) is a genuine shepherd's hut that's been prettily painted and decorated. Just big enough for a bed and a stove, it's in a cottage garden beside open fields, within easy reach of Brighton, and is aimed at walkers and cyclists. The Shepherd's Return (Sutton End, near Petworth; tel: 01798-869 364; www. theshepherdsreturn.com) offers a similar experience in a purpose-built hut. For something completely different, try The Big Green Bus (Whitesmith, near Lewes; www.biggreenbus. co.uk), a cleverly converted stationary double-decker with a kitchen and lounge downstairs and three bedrooms upstairs.

You'll find cosy bell tents, yurts and shepherd's huts at Knepp Safaris (New Barn Farm, near Horsham; tel: 01403-713 230; www.kneppsafaris. co.uk), where a re-wilding project offers 4WD safari drives and nature walks focused on wildflowers, trees, deer, birds or insects. At Glottenham Farm (Robertsbridge; tel: 07865-078 477; www.glottenham.co.uk), you can stay in one of four comfortable yurts and take courses in art, craft, wild cooking and bushcraft.

At Castle Cottage Tree House (Coates Castle, near Petworth; tel: 01798-865 001; www.castlecottage.info), a bohemian hideaway nestled in a sweet chestnut tree in the grounds of a grand gothic mansion, the owners a fix you up

Inside one of the cosy yurts at Knepp Safaris, near Horsham.

with guided walks and other activities. Bensfield Treehouse (Beech Hill, near Wadhurst; tel: 01348-830 922; www. bensfieldtreehouse.co.uk), a smart cabin with a rope bridge, polished floors and a modern kitchen, would make a good base for woodland and farmland walks. Swallowtail Hill Farm (Beckley, near Rye; 01797-260 890; www. swallowtailhill.com) has off-grid accommodation in two cute cabins and a pair of fairytale timber cottages; nature, photography or art walks can be arranged on request.

ART AND DESIGN

West Dean College (West Dean, near Chichester; tel: 01243-811 301; www.westdean.org.uk) offers residential short courses in creative skills including painting, dressmaking, millinery and stonemasonry. The setting is inspiring, with beautiful gardens.

Practical Information

GETTING THERE

By Road
The M23 motorway and a fan of A-roads (the A24, A23, A22, A26 and A21) lead south into Sussex from London and the M25. There's also access from the West Country via Salisbury, Southampton and the M27.

By Rail
Direct trains from London Victoria and Gatwick Airport will take you right into the centre of Brighton, Lewes, Eastbourne, Chichester, Hastings, Amberley and Arundel. For fares and timetables, contact National Rail Enquiries (tel: 08457-484 950; www.nationalrail.co.uk).

By Coach
National Express (tel: 0871-781 8181; www.nationalexpress.com) runs coaches from Victoria Coach Station in London to Arundel, Battle, Bexhill, Brighton, Chichester, Eastbourne, Hastings, Littlehampton and Seaford.

By Air
Gatwick Airport (tel: 0844-892 0322; www.gatwickairport.com) is around 27 miles (44km) north of Brighton. Regular direct train services link Gatwick to Brighton (28 mins), Lewes (37 mins), Eastbourne (55 mins), Arundel (49 mins) and Chichester (53 mins). Southampton Airport (tel: 0844-481 7777; www.southamptonairport.com) is 32 miles (52km) west of Chichester, connected by direct train (45 mins). Heathrow Airport (tel: 0844-335 1801; www.heathrow.com) is 64 miles (103km) from Brighton, served by direct National Express coach (2 hours and 20 mins) or by train via London.

By Sea
DFDS Seaways (www.dfdsseaways.co.uk) runs car and passenger ferries from Dieppe in northern France to Newhaven (4 hours; three daily May–Sept, two daily Oct–Apr). Ferries also operate from northern France and the Channel Islands to Portsmouth, which is linked to Sussex by rail.

By Cycle
National Cycle Routes to Sussex include Route 223 from Chertsey, Weybridge, Guildford and Horsham to Shoreham-by-Sea, Route 20 from South London, Croydon and Crawley to Brighton and Route 21 from Greenwich, Crawley, East Grinstead and Royal Tunbridge Wells to Eastbourne. For details, contact Sustrans (tel: 0117-926 8893; www.sustrans.org.uk).

Brighton Station is served by regular trains from London.

Buses outside Brighton Station.

GETTING AROUND

Bus and Coach

Brighton & Hove buses (tel: 01273-886 200; www.buses.co.uk) connect Brighton, Lewes, Seaford, Eastbourne, Devil's Dyke and Steyning. Stagecoach buses (tel: 0871-200 2233; www.stage coachbus.com) cover Eastbourne, Bexhill, Pevensey, Hastings and Rye. For details of buses around Chichester, Midhurst and Arundel, visit the West Sussex County Council website (www. westsussex.gov.uk). Bus drivers sell single tickets but if you're making more than two journeys a day, you can usually save money by buying a one-day or season ticket; Brighton & Hove Buses have a smartphone app for this.

Cycling

Sussex has a corker of a long-distance cycle route in the South Downs Way (www.nationaltrail.co.uk/south-downs-way), a 100-mile (160km) National Trail from Winchester to Eastbourne. National Cycle Route 2 (www. sustrans.org.uk) also runs through the region. It's not yet complete, but a satisfying section follows the seafront from Worthing to Cuckmere Haven, then curves inland. Elsewhere, there's a growing network of cycle paths. Brighton and Hove City Council has published a cycle map, available online (www.brighton-hove.gov.uk) and from tourist information points.

Rail

Three Bridges, Haywards Heath and Brighton are the hubs of the Southern railway network south of Gatwick Airport. From Brighton, there are regular train services to Lewes, Seaford, Southease, Glynde, Berwick and Eastbourne, where you can change for Pevensey Bay, Bexhill, Winchelsea and Rye. Heading west from Brighton, trains serve Littlehampton (for Arundel and Amberley), Chichester and Bosham. A Southern DaySave ticket (tel: 03451-272 920; www.southern railway.com) gives unlimited one-day travel on trains in Sussex. For fares and timetables, contact National Rail Enquiries (tel: 08457-484 950; www. nationalrail.co.uk).

Driving

Within Sussex, the main towns are linked by the A24, A23, A22, A26 and A21 running roughly north to south, the A272 running west to east along the Downs and the A27 parallel to the

Car-free Touring

With a little planning, you can reduce the environmental impact of your trip by leaving the car at home. The city tours featured in this book are designed to be followed on foot and many sections of our cross-country tours could be tackled by public transport or bike. Brighton & Hove bus route 12/12X, for example, covers parts of Tours 2, 6 and 7 (Kemptown, Rottingdean, Seaford, Cuckmere Haven and Eastbourne), while Stagecoach bus route 99 covers parts of Tours 7 and 8 (Eastbourne, Pevensey, Bexhill and Hastings). Travelling by train, you could visit Fishbourne, Chichester, Littlehampton, Arundel and Amberley (Tours 10, 9 and 12) in a single trip. To plan a journey via public transport, visit Traveline (www.traveline.info).

Opera fans at the annual Glyndebourne Festival Opera.

coast. The A259 from Chichester to Rye via Littlehampton, Brighton, Eastbourne, Bexhill and Hastings is a slower but scenic alternative to the A27, with fine views of the English Channel from several stretches. Away from the main roads, a web of country lanes leads from village to village. Access to holiday hotspots like Brighton and West Wittering is often congested on summer weekends.

Car Hire

Most car hire companies will only rent to 21–75 year olds with at least a year's experience of driving. In some cases the minimum age is 23. Firms with offices in Sussex include Avis (tel: 0808-284 5566; www.avis.co.uk); Enterprise (tel: 0800-800 227; www.enterprise.co.uk), Europcar (tel: 0871-384 1087; www.europcar.co.uk) and Hertz (tel: 0843-309 3099; www.hertz.co.uk).

Parking

In city centres, visitor parking is restricted to car parks and metered parking spaces. These are expensive by local standards and are often scarce. There is a free Park and Ride car park at Withdean (BN1 5JD) in Brighton, from which the bus fare includes unlimited travel on the Brighton & Hove network that day. Chichester operates a Park and Ride scheme during the Christmas shopping season. Smaller town centres typically allow free parking for limited periods.

FACTS FOR THE VISITOR

Disabled Travellers

Even though there's a high concentration of historic properties and gardens in Sussex, easy access is becoming the norm rather than the exception. Open Britain (tel: 0845-124 9971; www.openbritain.net), managed by the UK charity Tourism For All, provides information on accessible travel.

Emergencies
Fire, Ambulance, Police: tel: 999.
National Health Service: tel: 111.

Entertainment
Sussex offers a wealth of arts and entertainment, with Brighton's annual festival the second largest in Britain after Edinburgh. Glyndebourne Opera House, the Chichester Festival Theatre and the Brighton Dome present performances of world-class theatre, music, opera and dance, and there's also a thriving commercial, indie and fringe entertainment scene. Big name musicians and comedians appear at the larger venues and stars of the future often play gigs in Brighton's many pubs. Brighton also has an energetic club scene. For listings, check out www.visitsussex.org.

LGBT
Famed for its tolerance and inclusiveness, Brighton is a capital of lesbian, gay, bisexual and transgender culture. The area around St James's Street in Kemptown has the highest concentration of gay pubs, bars and shops, but individuals of all persuasions typically mingle throughout the city. In Eastbourne, The Hart (www.thehart.co.uk) is a popular LGBT pub.

Opening Hours
From Monday to Saturday, most shops open between 7.30am and 10am and close between 5.30am and 10pm. Supermarkets and convenience stores have the longest hours. City boutiques often open and close late. On Sundays, most large shops open for six hours in the middle of the day, with small shops often open for longer. Post offices and banks are closed on Saturday afternoons and Sundays. Last orders is 11pm except on Sundays, when it's usually earlier.

Tourist Information
The following centres provide free advice, maps, brochures and leaflets on sights and events. Some also offer a booking service for local accommodation, transport and attractions.

Arundel, Arundel Museum, Mill Road; tel: 01903-882 266; www.sussexbythesea.com.

Brighton, Brighton Centre, King's Road; tel: 01273-290 337; www.visitbrighton.com

Chichester, The Novium, Tower Street; tel: 01243-775 888; www.visitchichester.org.

Eastbourne, Cornfield Road; tel: 0871-663 0031; www.visiteastbourne.com.

Brighton Pride.

Accommodation

Sussex has no shortage of good places to stay. Just about every style of accommodation is covered, from grand seafront hotels to elegant boutique guesthouses and historic inns with low beams and open fires. For self-caterers, there are smart city or coastal apartments, cosy country cottages, rustic yurts and even treehouses (see page 126). Families have plenty of choice including upbeat resorts run by Butlins (www.butlins.com), Haven (www.haven.com), Hoseasons (www.hoseasons.co.uk) and Park Holidays (www.parkholidays.com).

During high season, July to September, it's wise to book ahead. Other busy times include Christmas, Easter, the Brighton Festival (May) and Lewes Bonfire Night (5 Nov).

You'll find accommodation listings on tourism websites such as Visit Sussex (www.visitsussex.org), Visit Brighton (www.visitbrighton.com), Visit Chichester (www.visitchichester.org) and, for the South Downs National Park, Our Land (www.our-land.co.uk/holidays/south-downs).

HOTELS AND B&BS

The price bands below are based on the cost of a standard en suite double room and breakfast for two people in high season.

£££ = over £200
££ = £125–200
£ = under £125

BRIGHTON

Artist Residence
33 Regency Square; tel: 01273-324 302; www.artistresidencebrighton.co.uk.
One of the most original of Brighton's many boutique hotels, this is a Regency townhouse that's been given a quirky 21st-century makeover. It's furnished with upcycled objects such as old crates, junkshop mirrors and vintage beds; tables, shelves and even shower doors are made from recycled timber. ££

Drakes
43–4 Marine Parade; tel: 01273-696 934; www.drakesofbrighton.com.
Perfect for a romantic seaside stay, this is an elegant double-fronted townhouse hotel, right on the Kemptown seafront. The styling is smart and contemporary and the best rooms have high ceilings, moulded cornices and huge windows with fabulous sea views. ££

Grand
97–9 King's Road; tel: 01273-224 300; www.grandbrighton.co.uk.
Behind the wedding-cake facade of Brighton's landmark hotel is an imposing lobby with a majestic staircase. The rooms, which are luxurious, have recently been re-styled in relaxing shades of soft pink, beige and turquoise. £££

LEWES

Berkeley House
2 Albion Street; tel: 01273-476 057; www.berkeleyhouselewes.com.
On one of Lewes' most beautiful streets, this townhouse B&B has smartly decorated rooms and beds so comfortable you'll sleep like a log. On warm days, you could have breakfast (full English, smoked salmon and scrambled eggs or waffles with fruit and cream) in the flint-walled courtyard garden. £

Pelham House
St Andrew's Lane; tel: 01273-488 600; www.pelhamhouse.com.
This substantial Georgian house is one of Lewes' most elegant places to stay, with spacious public areas and sympathetically modernised rooms. At the

back, the wisteria-draped brick facade opens onto a terrace and lawns dotted with daisies – a lovely setting for afternoon tea. ££

OUSE VALLEY, CUCKMERE VALLEY AND THE SUSSEX HERITAGE COAST

The Ram Inn

The Street, Firle; tel: 01273-858 222; www.raminn.co.uk.

The Ram is a country gastropub with four lovely guest rooms in the heart of Bloomsbury country. Decorated in soft, calm colours, the style is gently contemporary, blending vintage oddments with simple, modern lamps and bathroom fittings. The beds have soft duvets and Egyptian cotton sheets. £

Wingrove House

High Street, Alfriston; tel: 01323-870 276; www.wingrovehousealfriston. com.

With an unmatched choice of places to eat, drink and go walking or riding, the pretty village of Alfriston is one of the most appealing places to stay in the Sussex countryside. Wingrove House makes a stylish base – it's a romantic little hotel with elegant verandas and views of the church. ££

EASTBOURNE AND AROUND

Grand Hotel

King Edward's Parade, Eastbourne; tel: 01323-412 345; www.grandeast bourne.com.

This palatial Victorian hotel calls its humblest rooms Deluxe and its largest suite Presidential. All are comfortable, with traditional decor. Leisure facilities are first class, with a garden, pools, health club and access to the Royal Eastbourne Golf Club and David Lloyd leisure centre. ££

The Lamb Inn

Wartling, near Hailsham; tel: 01323-832 116; www.lambinnwartling.co.uk.
Climb the steep staircase in this attractive country pub and you'll find five small but cosy and reasonably priced rooms with en suite bathrooms or shower rooms. Herstmonceux Castle is just a mile and a half away. £

HIGH WEALD AND HASTINGS

The Griffin Inn

High Street, Fletching; tel: 01825-722 890; www.thegriffininn.co.uk.

The Griffin has everything you might wish for in a country pub – a cosy, historic interior, a well-kept garden,

One of the spacious rooms at Drakes.

great food, a sociable atmosphere and a pretty village setting with stunning views of Sheffield Park and the Ouse Valley. Its guest rooms have an attractive, cottagey style. £

Swan House

Hill Street, Hastings; tel: 01424-430 014; www.swanhousehastings.co.uk. This romantic B&B is so beautifully styled, it could give you serious home envy. It's a late 15th-century house with low ceilings, exposed timbers and a huge living room fireplace. The bedrooms are decorated in soft, tasteful neutral colours and have little surprises here and there – a boldly printed cushion, for example, or a pretty seashell mosaic. £

CHICHESTER AND AROUND

The Goodwood Hotel

Goodwood Estate; tel: 01243-927 082; www.goodwood.com.
Sizeable but not impersonal, this is a comfortable country house hotel. The rooms, which are found in the 18th-century part of the building and a more modern section, are mostly furnished in subtle, earthy shades and decorated with prints of race horses and the Goodwood Estate. The indoor swimming pool is attractive and there are extensive grounds to explore. £££

George Bell House

4 Canon Lane, Chichester; tel: 01243-813 586; www.chichestercathedral.org.uk.
Opportunities to stay in a cathedral close are rare indeed, so this 19th-century brick and flint B&B is very special. Its boutique style bedrooms provide accommodation for visiting clergy, with any remaining rooms available to others. Named after a former bishop who was a patron of the arts, the reception rooms feature paintings on loan from Pallant House. Parking is included. £

MIDHURST AND AROUND

The Church House

Church Hill, Midhurst; tel: 01730-812 990; www.churchhousemidhurst.com.
Created out of a cluster of 13th-century cottages, this gorgeous and characterful B&B brims with charm. The top floor suites are huge and glamorous, with soaring ceilings. A relaxed breakfast is served in the lovely, open plan living space. ££

The Old Railway Station

Station Road, Petworth; tel: 01798-342 346; www.old-station.co.uk.
This elegant timber pavilion was once considered the most beautiful railway station in Britain. Some time after the track was removed in 1966, the site was converted into a B&B. You can stay in the house or in an immaculately maintained early 20th-century Pullman carriage with mahogany interiors, inlaid with marquetry. £

ARUNDEL AND AROUND

Amberley Castle Hotel

Amberley Castle, Amberley; tel: 01798-831 992; www.amberleycastle.co.uk/hotel.
This gracious manor house hotel is tucked right inside Amberley's 14th-century castle walls. The grandest rooms have four-poster beds and open fires, and even the more modest rooms are comfortable and characterful, with exposed beams and leaded light windows. The grounds are enchanting, too, with peacocks and a treehouse to discover. £££

The Town House

65 High Street, Arundel; tel: 01903-883 847; www.thetownhouse.co.uk.
The first floor suite in this slender Regency house has an ornate ceiling and tall windows opening onto a balcony; the double room above has a four-poster bed and views of Arundel Castle. The remaining three rooms are cosy and affordable. £

Index

Credits

Insight Guides Great Breaks Brighton, Sussex & the South Downs
Editor: Rachel Lawrence
Author: Emma Gregg
Head of Production: Rebeka Davies
Picture Editor: Tom Smyth
Cartography: Carte
Photo credits: Alamy 13, 33, 34L, 48/49, 108B; Corrie Wingate/Apa Publications 7TR, 61, 67, 104, 105; Dan Dennison/Brighton Festival 30ML; Getty Images 4/5, 6MC, 7T, 7M, 10, 14/15, 16, 20/21, 21, 22, 26, 32, 35, 40, 43, 44, 45, 54, 57, 58, 59, 62/63T, 62B, 64, 72, 76/77, 83, 87, 90TL, 95, 96, 99, 100, 101, 102, 108T; iStock 36/37, 37, 41, 42, 50, 55, 56, 65, 66, 78, 79, 84, 92, 106; Photoshot 94; Public domain 90ML, 90/91T; Shutterstock 6MC, 7M, 7BR, 51, 81, 86, 88, 97, 107; Steve Cutner/Apa Publications 6ML, 11, 17, 23; Tom Smyth 80; Victor Frankowski/Brighton Festival 30TL, 30/31T; VisitEngland 6ML, 8/9, 47; VisitEngland/1066 Country 73; VisitEngland/Diana Jarvis 52T, 52B; VisitEngland/Luke Rogers 74; VisitEngland/Visit Brighton 18, 24, 26/27, 38; VisitEngland/Visit Eastbourne 7MR, 69; VisitEngland/Visit Eastbourne/Towner Gallery 71; VisitEngland/VisitBrighton 25
Cover credits: Shutterstock (main) iStock (BL&BR)

No part of this book may be reproduced, stored in a retrieval system or transmitted in any form or means electronic, mechanical, photocopying, recording or otherwise, without prior written permission from APA Publications.

CONTACTING THE EDITORS:
Every effort has been made to provide accurate information in this publication, but changes are inevitable. The publisher cannot be responsible for any resulting loss, inconvenience or injury. We would appreciate it if readers would call our attention to any errors or outdated information. We also welcome your suggestions; please contact us at: hello@insightguides.com

Information has been obtained from sources believed to be reliable, but its accuracy and completeness, and the opinions based thereon, are not guaranteed.

First Edition 2016
Printed in China by CTPS

Worldwide distribution enquiries:
APA Publications (Singapore) Pte, 7030 Ang Mo Kio Avenue 5, 08-65 Northstar @ AMK, Singapore 569880; apasin@singnet.com.sg
Distributed in the UK and Ireland by:
Dorling Kindersley Ltd, A Penguin Group company, 80 Strand, London, WC2R 0RL; sales@uk.dk.com
Distributed in the US by:
Ingram Publisher Services, 1 Ingram Boulevard, PO Box 3006, La Vergne, TN 37086-1986; ips@ingramcontent.com
Distributed in Australia & New Zealand by:
Woodslane, 10 Apollo St, Warriewood, NSW 2102, Australia; info@woodslane.com.au